Meadowlark

Judi Loren Grace

Stansbury Publishing
Chico, California

Published by Stansbury Publishing
Chico, California

Other works by Judi Loren Grace:
The Third Floor, Judi Loren Grace
Dreamscape in A minor, Judi Loren Grace
Rita's Road, Judi Loren Grace
Meadowlark, Judi Loren Grace

 Follow Judi Loren Grace on Facebook
www.jetstreampublishing.com

© 2016 Judi Loren Grace, all rights reserved.

ISBN: 9781935807230
Library of Congress Control Number: 2016948087

Printed in the United States of America

This book is a work of fiction. References to real people, events, establishments, or locales are intended only to provide a sense of authenticity and are used ficticiously. All characters and all incidents and dialogue is drawn from the author's imagination and are not to be construed as real.

Contents

ACKNOWLEDGEMENTS AND DEDICATION		V
PROLOGUE		1
ONE	THE RIGHT MOVES	3
TWO	REWIND	11
THREE	SECLUSION	23
FOUR	PROFESSIONAL KIDNAPPERS	33
FIVE	EXPOSED	41
SIX	LIVING A LIE	53
SEVEN	GRACIOUS NEIGHBOR	67
EIGHT	SNOW AND ASH	75
NINE	BROKEN GLASS	87
TEN	UNDERCOVER	93
ELEVEN	BLENDING OUR LOVE	103
TWELVE	COWGIRL UP	121
THIRTEEN	THE FILE	135
FOURTEEN	THE LONE STAR STATE	143
FIFTEEN	CHANGES	149
SIXTEEN	A FATHERS CONFESSION	161
SEVENTEEN	WEDDING BELLS	179
EIGHTEEN	SAYING GOODBYE	187
NINETEEN	GROWING PAINS	193
TWENTY	BLUEBONNETS	207
TWENTY-ONE	NETTIE REFLECTS	221
TWENTY-TWO	CROSSROADS	231
TWENTY-THREE	THE TABLES TURN	239
TWENTY-FOUR	OLD FRIENDS	257
TWENTY-FIVE	TURN OF EVENTS	265
TWENTY-SIX	FATHERS UNITE	275
TWENTY-SEVEN	BREEZY DAY	293
EPILOGUE		297

Acknowledgements

Connie Ballou Back Alley Graphics–cover art, design and interior layout
Chris Calloway–proof reading and suggestions.
Dennis Connor–retired Spanish teacher and friend, helped with Spanish phrases and spelling. Gracias mi querido amigo.
Nancy's Bookshelf–thank you for your faithful radio interviews on KCHO 91.7
Dan Barnett–thank you for your ongoing reviews and reports in the *Chico* Enterprise Record.

Dedication

On occasion, when a shadow crosses your path it stays with you forever. This story is dedicated these magnificent shadows. Thank you for your display of integrity and strength.

Mary Rogers, Cassie Hansen PhD, Ingrid Norlie, Janet Wright MD, Brittany Woodcox, daughter Dana Brooke, Lisa Boettger, Janet Mills Elliott, Jen Wilkinson, and Susan Rozier.

These men listed below are the shadows of all shadows, and they always keep their light on the path.

Son Spencer Adkisson, Jason Finney, Laurie Norton, John Hansen, Brian Boettger, Sal Cordero, Len Stachelek, Roger Graves PhD. and Lonon Smith

Listen to the older generation,
for they have lived life and experienced
more than you can imagine.
But never discount the younger ones,
for they have ideas and a fresh outlook.

Prologue

LOOKING BACK FROM MY PERCH, I close my eyes and reconstruct the day, the exact moment it all began to unfold and rear its ugly head. A split second decision, with good intentions combined with natural instincts that most humans have. This is the switch that moved my life to another realm. My simple life as I had known it began to swirl in all directions the moment I touched her.

This new existence I now live is contrary to how I was raised and erupts into a constant battle inside my head that cautions me about right and wrong. A life I never imagined is laid out before me. The unexpected left turn began the day I stepped out of the shadows from the safety of my front porch and met head on a world of drugs violence and evil.

Blending in with the walls has always been my refuge. It's a comfortable and secure place to live, at least I thought it was until I realized how the old tapes in my head still run freely and play; ignorance is bliss. I was taught to color inside the lines, never talk back, and to be gracious under all circumstances. These subliminal messages from childhood play back in my mind throughout the day. Remember child: stay in the shadows, be seen and not heard, and always glide through life unnoticed and detached. It's the safest route.

CHAPTER ONE

The Right Moves

NATURALLY, I DID WHAT ALL GOOD GIRLS DO; after college I married my one and only sweetheart, Jim. We bought a vintage house and had it restored to our liking. Our first home sits on a grassy knoll with huge maple trees surrounding the property. Like most young couples, we get a dog, a sweet Golden Retriever we name Izzy. Life is playing out as it should, perfect.

Standing tall at 5'1" I am always described as short in stature. Most people talk over my head as if I am a child. Jim's family is concerned that we will produce short stocky sons. I resent this accusation, but never let on that I think they are a shallow bunch of bigots.

I have black hair with green eyes and a dimple in my chin. I suppose I could pass for *cute,* but I wish I had a few more inches of height and not such a plain Jane face. I've worn my hair in a fluffy bubble since third grade, and with that came the responsibility and daily chore of keeping it nice and tidy because moist weather makes it appear to be a curly tossed salad. For some reason Jim likes me, and he is attracted

CHAPTER ONE

to me. He says he likes my smile, my patience, my ability to listen and grasp information laid out before me. He likes my hair and eyes; he likes the food I prepare and says we are a good match. We are both calm, matter of fact individuals. I use this term *individual* ever so lightly as I have never really seen myself as a full-grown adult.

In our marriage I have no regrets, our life is serene and peaceful. I have made my nest and now dwell in a comfortable place known as denial. This feeling of denial begins to bubble to the surface after I make the decision to become a woman with an opinion, listen to my inner being, and follow my heart.

We were married just a few years when our daughter Dana Bea arrived on the scene. She rattled our cage a bit, but slowly she developed her own personality and began to blend in with her parents. She is her dad; calm, quiet and attentive, she has an inner strength that must come from his side of the family. I spend most of my mothering days staring at her face taking in her scent and marveling at the beauty we created. It is a life to cherish.

I'm the only surviving member of my immediate family. My parents were killed in a head-on collision one New Year's Eve. There was more ice than snow, and they skidded across the road into oncoming traffic.

I remember my sister; the night we were orphaned. She was so excited for our parents to return home that fateful night. Funny, this memory is quite vivid. To this day, my mind periodically goes there. Abigale had waited patiently on the couch in the living room; calmly she waited, looking out from between the drapes for their car lights to come down the driveway between a line of trees that stood tall, reaching to the sky, and leading the way home. I can still see her today, her body making a lump behind the tapestry drapes. She is hunched over the couch behind the drapes, and she waits. Finally, we were forced to go to bed, ushered upstairs by our sitter.

Our sitter got the phone call sometime during the night and followed instructions. She phoned our grandparents. An old aunt and uncle we hardly knew rushed over to stay with us, told us the news emphasizing that the accident was fast and our parents didn't suffer, then added that they aren't sure what to do with us.

Our older, extended family had a late night meeting tossing around ideas while two little girls listen, clinging tight to each other. I was eight, my sister ten. We were raised the next ten years by our loyal and conservative grandparents, who loved us, doted on us and felt sorry for us. They also wanted us to grow up quickly and go off to college so they could retire. Their demeanor was enough to let us know they did not want to raise a second family.

My older sister Abigale and I had to live with our mother's parents the remainder of our youth, until we each turned eighteen. We both received high scores on our grades, because we instinctively knew we had to study hard to get into college if we ever wanted to relax and breathe again. We both knew we had to continue on with our lives, without the love and comfort of our parents. Living together away from our staunch grandparents' watchful eyes was our main goal. College was the exit door out of our dry, controlled environment.

Like me, my big sister had dark hair, but hers was always easier to control. She was a sweet girl and through the years she opened the

CHAPTER ONE

doors into womanhood with numerous late night conversations about love and life. She had a natural talent with her hair, and she knew how to carry herself. She told me, "Never slump." She explained about coming of age, and boys, and she also gently teased me when I began to mature and look more like a woman. She advised me when to speak and when to listen, she never wanted me to get into trouble with our grandparents. Abigale kept her arm around me as an older trusted sister would, and together we lived and relied on each other for security.

My beloved sister died at the tender age of twenty-four, due to complications in childbirth. Her only child, a premature baby boy, died in her arms. Abigale died a few days later due to hemorrhaging. Her husband never looked back. He gutted their home, sold most of their belongings and moved across the United States. I suppose in some grief stricken way he blamed her for the death of his only son. I have never seen him since. He left me a few photos and Abby's wedding dress.

Losing my sister made me want to establish a secure home and a lasting bond with my own family. Now, as I sit next to my daughter and watch her movements and expressions, I secretly wish I looked more like her. She is tall like her dad and has dark brown hair with a glint of red. She has bright green eyes, like me, but with heavy brows that she uses to her advantage; keeping them waxed with a very sexy high arch to frame her face and high cheekbones. Some days Dana Bea reminds me of her father and sometimes I see flashes of Abby.

I miss having a sister so much my heart aches. I do wonder, and always will, what Abby would have looked like as she aged, if we would have aged in the same way, in looks and body. I also wonder how her life would have unfolded had she lived. I can only assume it would not be as messed up as mine.

THE RIGHT MOVES

Dana Bea has my strong will, and we have similar shaped eyes and smiles. I am heavenly in love with her smooth peaceful manner and the aura that surrounds her being. My husband has the same effect on me with his sweetness. My sister had mothered me. This is who I am today, a mix of many influences.

My husband Jim is slender, he loves to walk five miles every morning and is in amazingly good health. Time continues to pass by and his once dark hair has started to gray on the sides, this only adds to his striking good looks. Sometimes in the evening he sits in his leather chair, lights his pipe and has a bourbon on the rocks. I watch him and feel satisfied as we progress in age and in our relationship.

I *supported* us during Jim's grad school years. With the help of his grandparents' trust we continued to glide through life. My role as his wife is to make our home his sanctuary. Keeping my part-time secretarial job in a large financial firm is a must, it supplies me with breathing room. I tell myself that I work to help us live debt free and not be obliged to anyone. My insistence on working actually comes from my independent thinking, this is directly related to being orphaned and raised by relatives who clearly didn't want to raise two little girls.

Jim is financially successful due to his knowledge of stocks and skilled investments, but we both are growing restless and bored. A year after our daughter's high school graduation we decide that we are financially secure enough to relocate to a small town called Dunsmuir and semi-retire. I give notice at my job—*my life-line*. Jim assures me how wonderful it will be to stay home and daydream of travel.

My husband isn't still for long. He takes a position as a consultant, providing us with supplemental income. We don't need the money,

CHAPTER ONE

but he needs to use his mind. I felt from the beginning his crazy idea to move and semi-retire in our forties was premature. I regret leaving my job. He reminds me that our stocks are strong, slow and steady, our house is paid for, and our daughter is away at college. His part-time job is just for fun.

My boring life magnifies and morphs into a lovely locked cage. I move along in a state of repetitive movements.

Jim is always quiet, reading and researching stocks, he is a constant object in our home. Although, not exactly a warm fuzzy object, he is my security and friend. He loves to research new opportunities. Sometimes he goes outside into the garage and tinkers with wood-working projects and putters with gadgets. He is a content gentle man. We go for long walks through the woods with our dog and *everything is bliss*. Translation—we are secure.

I didn't realize my strength until one leisurely Sunday afternoon in the fall. The trees are changing color and the colorful leaves threaten to cover our lawn. The stillness and pleasant feeling of security is what I remember most about this day. Sitting in my comfortable overstuffed chair I relaxed in my usual state of denial. This particular afternoon while sitting together in our living room, I recall the atmosphere was as normal and peaceful as one can imagine. Suddenly my life changed, like the snap of a finger.

The shock of watching my husband gasp for breath and cry out in pain gives me a start, and I freeze in place without thought. He grabs his chest and crumples forward, falling head first out of his wing back chair into a heap on our carpeted floor. I am numb and not responding as quickly as I should. It seems to take forever before I dive off my chair to reach him. I am watching this scene unfold failing to understand the magnitude before I leap. I reach him and cradle his head in my arms. I rock and pet his limp body lying there in a fetal position. In a panic I reach for the phone and dial the ambulance while my love, my rock, my life, sleeps for eternity. Jim dies in my arms.

Time seems to move in slow motion, like honey from a cold cabinet; you watch and wait, hit the bottom to give it a boost and finally it slowly slides out. I still have Buddy, our dog from our first golden retriever, Izzy. I baby Buddy and have all the time in the world to pet him and walk him, this becomes a daily morning ritual. The days continue to pass by ever so slowly. It has been one year since my life took this sharp turn. I stew over things, one being the small child around the corner.

Our daughter Dana Bea graduates from college this May. I don't have the energy to fly there, and certainly not to drive, but of course I do—*for her*. I load up Buddy and drive south on the coastal highway until I reach San Luis Obispo. I am here to cheer her on. I wear a sun hat and a nice dress, but my heart beats with sadness. The music plays and the graduates file in. I am a wet mess, and the tears run down my cheeks as I see her with her classmates. I cry happy tears for her achievements and hard work, and sad tears for her father's absence. There she is in a sea of caps and gowns. Finally, her name is called and she walks across the stage with a wide grin, shakes hands with the Dean and receives her diploma. I stand and clap with such passion I feel I am too loud and lost in pride. I may have made too much noise, and slowly retreat back down to my seat with purpose.

CHAPTER ONE

We celebrate with a great lunch, great wine and a walk downtown. We talk about life, her future and all of the things she wants to accomplish. I stay a week with my daughter and my dog, then sadly, Buddy and I say goodbye and head north.

I begin to make positive changes. I go to my first yoga class, buy all new stretchy yoga clothes and a mat. I try new recipes. I paint the entire inside of my home using more feminine colors throughout, and I put lots of girly things around the place. But you can't control fate and it was during this time of healing that Buddy became ill and the vet could not save him. I have to face the sad chore of burying my Buddy in our backyard. I dig his grave by myself and Dana Bea sends flowers.

CHAPTER TWO

Rewind

LIFE IS NOT GOING WELL THESE DAYS. I want to put our *forever* home on the market and purchase a smaller place that feels cozy, with less square footage. I'd like to have a more retro feel to my next home. What I actually want is to run away from Buddy's grave. But I gather my senses and decide this house is perfect. It sits on the outskirts of the forest. It is idyllic, and besides, Jim found it and this is where I am supposed to be, up here in the North State, in Dunsmuir, dead dog and all.

Our home is tucked up in the mountains, in a small town with less traffic, and less fuss. I fear my choice to stay here, alone, away from my daughter is anti-social behavior. I am a five-hour drive from her and miss her terribly, staying up here seems totally un-motherly, but I have to stay. I have to find inner peace. I have to thaw out, and find myself without Jim.

Dana Bea drives up frequently to visit, eat her mom's cooking and enjoy the outdoors. We hike together and cook together. In the winter months she flies in to the nearest airport, rents a car and settles in for a week of rest, pampering and snow skiing. She and I have always enjoyed our time together. We like to show off our kitchen talents as each of us makes great sauces and salads, and I, without fail, put together her favorite childhood casserole dishes. Our conversations are soft, as if we don't want to disturb the dead, or shake away our mood and the natural sweet chemistry we share.

Our peaceful mood is broken by sounds in the distance of a baby wailing, crying, and screaming while a man's loud voice spits out venom. This is beginning to happen with frequency. One such night I urge my daughter to walk with me around the block just to see what is going on with this baby. "How do you feel about snooping a little?"

She is as intrigued as I am; she turns on a dime, runs to the hall closet and grabs two jackets. We slip on our darkest ski coats; plop on dark knit hats and on instinct I grab a camera. We step lightly and with caution into the night and walk to the end of the street, zipping up our collars and pulling down our caps. We turn right and walk along two snow sprinkled lawns, another right and past another few yards puts us on the other corner, staring at the home where all the screams are coming from. We stand and look at this house of evil. We walk out of the tree shadows cast by the moon with purpose and try not to look suspicious.

The unsightly house is around the corner from my home; thankfully, a two-story house sits between us. We take visual inventory of a battered car, ripped curtains, and open windows despite a severe drop in the nightly temperature. I notice that the crying had ceased and this is a huge relief. The yard is full of clutter and car parts. Empty cans toss about with the wind; there are weeds and broken glass—not a safe environment for a child. Dana Bea puts my camera up to her eye and snaps a photo, then slowly lowers the camera when we both notice the orange glint from a cigarette. Someone is watching us. It's the angry man. I have a good memory and memorize the license plate. Dana Bea snaps another picture, we turn and briskly walk away.

He steps out from his driveway and yells at us, "Is there a problem?"

Dana Bea, who stands six feet tall and has a skier's strong body, snaps her head quickly to the left and replies, "Oh, hi, sorry for disturbing you. We just love your car, my uncle used to drive us to school in one just like it."

He changes like a chameleon and is overjoyed with this pack of lies and tells liar Dana Bea the history of its ownership. He takes a long slow drag on his cigarette and goes on to tell us how he ended up with this particular prize car and what his plans are for restoring it. And of course, the value. We act impressed, in awe, and wish him well on his car adventure and investment. We wave goodbye and walk with imitation confidence to the top of the road, turn right and walk around the next corner and head down the gentle decline to my house. Both of us are shaking from fright and shivering from the chill of the night. We pick up speed and rush back to the safety of my home.

The night air is crisp, cold and quiet. I tell my daughter that while she was talking to that creepy guy, I was staring at a toddler who was watching us through the open window. "We made eye contact; it was mesmerizing. There is actually no glass, it is just casing, just a square where a window once held glass, what do you think about that honey?"

Surprised, she ignores my question, "You saw a toddler?"

CHAPTER TWO

"Yes I did, just standing there, watching us, staring at me while you were talking to that guy. This little child stared at me the entire time. She must have been freezing. She stood still and paralyzed like a mannequin. The toddler didn't move or blink; it was truly haunting."

The next day over morning coffee and banana nut bread we sit in silence. We begin to talk at the same time, about the dark uneasy feeling we each carry around on this clear crisp day. Dana Bea cautions me about safety measures, alerts me to tread lightly and offers other advice I should take. She repeats, "And no more walks around the block alone Mom; your neighbor seems a little off."

I wholeheartedly agree and promise to keep quiet. Dana Bea has frown lines across her forehead and appears worried as we sip our morning coffee and continue to chew the warm bread. We sit and numbly stare out the bay window towards the forest. Inside my heart, I sense enormous fear for this child.

Dana Bea grabs her bags near the door, turns around, puts them down, walks back to me and engulfs me with one of her bear hugs before she heads up the mountain to the ski lodge.

When she returns in the late afternoon we say nothing about our encounter, just lay round, eat and have hot tea. We are void of our normal easy conversation after our evening trek. The next morning, we say our goodbyes, hug and I sense her uneasiness about leaving me alone.

I have no idea just how incredibly strong my daughter's conviction will prove to play out in the coming months. She will be my rock and voice of reason. She is a force to be reckoned with.

REWIND

The Holidays whiz by and winter closes in while Christmas trees are tossed away with annoyance, or carried off to a side yard. Standing on my porch I hear sounds of celebration for the incoming year fill the night air. This new fresh year is one I shall never forget.

When I wake up tomorrow morning it will be a new year, a new beginning, 1984 is the year when my life as I once knew it changes forever, a change no one could ever imagine.

The phone rings, it is a cheerful and familiar voice wishing me a Happy New Year, Dana Bea happily says she is on her way back up North to stay with me during her last week of the holiday season. Once again she is here, pulling into the driveway. I am overjoyed and smiling like a little girl. We curl up together under a blanket and entwine our legs, my sweet girl and I, remembering years past. The room fills with the aroma of hot cider, and old memories fill our conversation. She mentions her father, and wishes he was here. I agree, and know that tomorrow morning she will rise, eat breakfast and snow ski without a care in the world—life goes on. She is the comfort I need, she grounds me. Even though I seem confident and calm, and feel healthy in my yoga pants, I am distant by choice.

Inside I feel my body scream and shake. She has no idea how horrible it is to hear this child scream out in pain. She only heard the cries once, and she felt helpless, but I hear it almost nightly.

Despite it all, Dana Bea and I enjoy our time together. There is simply something wonderful and magical about having my only child home. She blows life back into the house. We never mention the neighbor or the battered child from her last visit. I don't want her to think I

CHAPTER TWO

am over reacting due to loneliness, or prone to exaggeration, and I am fearful she won't want to come up north to visit me if I drag her into this crazy drama.

Some days I ride up to the lodge with her and watch the skiers. I sit on the deck bundled up and try to spot her as she traverses down the slope. Sometimes I have a bowl of chili with saltine crackers and sip hot tea. In the evening, we can hear the child, not every night, but many nights. The week sadly comes to an end and we bear hug and rock back and forth, while we take in each other's scent, then followed by the forever goodbye wave. I slowly walk back inside to enjoy the warmth of my home, but with a sense that a storm is brewing and it's not the weather.

The next time I hear the baby wail in pain, the mother bear comes out in me and I prepare for a full on change. Every cell in my body is on high alert. The cries are due to torture and continue to pull me towards my natural instincts. I know I must do the right thing. This is the moment I realize I must shed my exterior unemotional veneer and reach deep into my soul and stop this madness. The screams and cries continue, and the pitiful sounds seem to fly down the street and into my yard. I am getting up my nerve to interact and call the authorities.

One evening after the night quiets down, I step outside onto on my front porch. I thought I heard something hit the side of the house. I stand and stare down the street in either direction. I wonder if my other neighbors hear. How many of us listen and do nothing? I then realize that most of these homes are second homes, a place to enjoy a quiet peaceful get away. My neighbors are all part-time residents, as the locals call them, fair-weather summer neighbors.

Then I see it, the amber glow of his cigarette. He has been watching me from the shadows from a clump of pines on the corner. Immediately my body reacts with cold chills that race up my spine and the hair on the back of my neck stands on end. I am frightened and in slow motion take the sashes and pull my robe in nice and tight around my waist making a knot to match the one in my stomach. He is holding a stick, and he begins to smack it into the palm of his hand. He steps out to expose himself as a spineless wimp and begins to yell from his pine hideout.

"You seen my kid?" he demands.

I choke out, "No I haven't."

He smacks his palm a few times and yells in his loud smoky angry voice, "Girl, you better come out, girl, girl, I said GIRL!"

He walks away and I can hear him down the street and around the corner, yelling as he swats his palm.

I carefully move to the edge of the porch to see which way he went. I hear the continuous swats on the palm of his hand in the distance. I hope he continues to walk into the night and tumble right off a cliff. To make sure he is still walking away, I step down one step when I spot something, a slow movement out of the corner of my eye, a very slight shuffle. I wonder if the wind blew a kid's soccer ball under my tree. The cold night air moves it in the wind. I squat to look under the rail and look closely, squinting my eyes, and decide it is a patterned ball of tan and black—a ball that moves under my dogwood tree.

From the shelter of my front porch, I gingerly step out onto the fresh light blanket of snow, and look both ways for signs of the scary angry

CHAPTER TWO

man. I step onto the lawn and make my way to the edge of the house. My curiosity has the best of me and takes over logic. I hope this is not a trap. There, curled up, I recognize it as a small child, it's not a ball, it is her rump moving in tight to help her hide and stay warm. The pattern I see as I take a closer look is dirt on her little diaper and a long sleeve shirt. I scoop her up into my arms, and she crawls inside my robe for warmth and shelter. Her legs wrap around my hips, and her arms find their way inside and snuggle in a tight fold between our bodies.

Quickly I dash up the steps, huffing from lack of exercise and from fright of being seen. Just four more steps and we are inside. I make sure the curtains are closed tight. Still cradling her in my arms, we sit down on the thick shag carpet in front of the fireplace. Slipping out of my chenille robe, I gently place it around her shoulders and cover her little freezing legs.

There we sit. She squirms deeper into my chest, and I hold her tight, then lay us back and together we curl up together on the carpet in front of the roaring fire. We hold on to each other and I notice her swollen blackened eye, and she has a gash across her forehead. I lay with her, still wrapped inside of my robe and carry her into my bedroom, there I lay her on the bed, then grab Dana Bea's soft fluffy blanket out of my cedar chest, and I take some other baby blankets out of a bottom drawer, step back to her and put them around her to help her thaw out, thinking, "You just can't have enough blankets."

Back into the living room, we lay together and bond. Seems like an hour or so when I decide to scoop her up and walk towards the old caned rocker. She relaxes into my arms and accepts the warmth from all of the soft cotton blankets so long ago quilted with love. The rocker creaks and the sound fills the room as I gently pull her in nice and close, like the delicate treasure she is. I whisper, "Hello sweetheart, it's okay." I rub her feet, legs, arms and face as she begins to warm up, and I watch her eyes slowly close.

I lay her down in the center of my bed then push it towards the wall, moving her to safety with the bed tight in the corner.

I then realize she might need a clean diaper. This reality check puts me into high gear. I make sure she is secure and cozy, then run into the kitchen and begin to fold my kitchen towel into a triangle. I grab two safety pins from the top drawer in my desk, and run back into the bedroom with the towel and a damp warm washcloth. She doesn't wake or move a muscle as I wash her bottom and fuss with this cumbersome towel with an art design of strawberries on it as I fumble to make it fit between her little legs and bottom and hope it is comfortable.

I check out my handy work, slide in bed next to her and hope for the best when sunrise peeks through the curtains.

The next morning, she doesn't seem afraid as I assumed she would be. I closed my eyes last night and prepared mentally for wails of fright. She is a crier after all, I've heard her, and anticipate she'll wake up as a wild untamed animal. She lies awake in the soft bedding as quiet as a little mouse, while her eyes watch me, and then dart around the room. I ask her if she would like something to eat, and she stares back into my eyes. Out of lack of any other reason except intuition, I smile back and repeat, "Sweetheart, let's eat some yummy food."

I scoop her up into my arms and off we go into the kitchen. My first thought is how do I cook oatmeal with a child balanced on my hip. "Well now let's see …" I sit her down in a wing back chair, under a furry blanket and pull the chair to the opening of the kitchen. All is

CHAPTER TWO

well, and she seems pleased to watch. I realize at this time I have not changed her diaper. I smile and think, "Oh hell." I pull out another of my cute kitchen towels, fold it into a triangle, pick her up, and off we go back to the bedroom. I lay her on the bed and dig back into the cedar chest and find two mismatched diaper pins, one is a yellow duckling, the other one is a pink bow. I put a warm clean cloth on her bottom and clean her up, and think, "Next time I will sprinkle corn starch on her diaper rash." She is clean, and ready for breakfast. I take a step into the kitchen and think to myself, "What are you doing, have you gone mad?"

With a full tummy of warm oatmeal and milk, I run the bath water in the sink and give her a warm, well needed soapy cleansing; using my new rose soap Dana Bea had given me. She arches her back away from my soapy hands and this is the moment I witness the full scale of her scars and open flesh wounds across her back, arms and buttocks. The bruises on her arms and the gash on the side of her eye are concerning also. Her rump is black and blue. My heart sinks, and I have to concentrate so I don't throw up. My soapy hand covers my mouth as I witness true evil. She is rinsed off and wrapped in a warm soft cotton towel, and together we rock as I contemplate my next move. She drifts off to sleep and I carry her into the bedroom, lay her safely down in the center of the bed, then dash into the guest room and grab my Instamatic camera. A sense of clarity from the shock of her torturous life tells me to set this camera down. I dart back to the closet and retrieve Jim's Polaroid. I am afraid to take film exposing her heinous wounds to be developed at the drug store. I'd be arrested when I went back to pick up the film. This other camera seems the best and safest way to capture her wounds, fresh and previous, one day her tormenter and his abuse will be exposed.

REWIND

Carefully and gently I roll her over to her side and onto her tummy. She is in a deep sleep and lets out a restful sigh. I begin to snap the truth. I snap pictures of old wounds, now scars and fresh open sores and slashes. I take photos of her face, arms and hands, her black and blue bottom and the back and sides of her little legs. With each photo I have to wait and count to 15, then the photo will eject out of the camera to expose the truth. I reach for a pen on my nightstand and date the bottom of each photo, then set them on my dresser in a row to cure.

I curl up next to her, still in my robe and think, really think, the kind of deep thinking that edges on hysterics while your brain keeps repeating and swirling the same questions over and over, "What is happening, what are you doing, and why are you doing this? Be very careful."

I continue to help mend this child as I push forward trying to remember normal. She once again naps, so I take advantage of this moment to carefully and gently apply medicine, an anti-bacterial gel onto her wounds.

CHAPTER THREE

Seclusion

THE FIFTH DAY ARRIVES AND THEN NEXT. The sun goes down, then the next day drifts into our bedroom. I am exhausted from sleeping with one eye open, and caring for this precious child. I prepare for her to cut loose and begin to scream or be a crazy little girl, so I can witness why her father beat her. But she never does. The days are full with cooking, rocking, playing, and I am consumed and busy cutting up most of my kitchen towels. My thoughts have become more realistic; I have been caring for a missing child for five days and am certain this rescue and love time will be referred to as kidnapping in a court of law. I am fairly certain I will end up in a women's state penitentiary for 15-20 years. "Oh Jim, where are you honey? please help me, please, I beg of you, please send a message. Someone please help me with my next move. Who has sent this child to me?" She continues to nap and enjoy the love, while I prepare for life behind bars.

One thing is missing, odd actually. Over these last two weeks the media's lack of attention to this missing child is shocking. There is nothing in the local paper, no mention of a missing child on the news.

CHAPTER THREE

Nothing. Are the parents afraid of being caught as unfit, and possibly using drugs, besides beating a child? Are they afraid of a house search, the police or jail time? Or do they think a bear dragged her from her crib and through the open window, into the woods and ate her? I realize that the parents have not notified the police for a reason.

In the cover of pre-dawn darkness, I scoop up the child while she sleeps, lay her in the back seat, surround her with pillows then quickly drive to a nearby market. I lock the car doors and run in to grab a few necessities. She does not wake up and we are safely home before daylight. I am grateful the store owner is open early while he stocks his shelves. Unfortunately this retirement community store does not carry many of the items I need.

Dana Bea phones again and I assure her I'm fine. "No, your mother is great, yes, there's new snow, and no more problems with the yelling neighbor. It's all quiet and my life is repetitive as usual. Boring actually."

She suspects something is amiss and begins to dig. She wants to come home for a visit the first part of February.

I tell her, "No, no, that's okay."

She repeats, "No!" and asks, "What is wrong with you, are you tied up? Is he in the house? Are you sick, confused? Did you have a stroke?"

Her questions make me let out a guilty giggle, both from lying to my daughter for the first time ever and from her absurd questions. With a deep breath, I change my mind replying, "Yes, come up yes, yes, please do come, visit me." I think to myself, "Lets' just get this over with."

"Dana Bea, we have much to talk about." I reassure her, "I am just being a weirdo, changing my mind and all." She giggles with uncertainty. Her boring mother who has been a rock to all, the housekeeper, the laundress, the chef, wife, mother and the household accountant is not acting right.

I am unhinged. My daughter agrees, and says she'll be on her way to visit very soon. I have less than one month to muster up a plan, appear normal and in control of this absurd situation, and explain with confidence the obvious presence of my new roommate who toddles around with my kitchen towel as a diaper.

It's February, Dana Bea pulls up to my house in her new hatchback style car, with a rack on the top for snow skies. She steps out of the new snazzy car, looks around, and grabs her luggage. My heart pounds with each step she takes through the new snow. I walk out onto the porch, open my arms and we hug. Then, out of nowhere, I experience a breakdown, laying my head against her chest, she pats my back. I take a deep breath while she leads me back into the warmth of my home and out of the crispy air. The stress of the last month aids in my meltdown plus fatigue, fright, excitement, and lack of sleep. She rubs my shoulders and the back of my head while she ushers me towards the rocking chair. But I've had enough rocking for the moment. I stand up straight, turn and sit next to her on the couch, then have a good cry. Dana Bea hands a hankie to me with her long outstretched arm. I look at her and our eyes meet. It is time to confess.

CHAPTER THREE

We sit, I wipe my face and we don't say a word. I try to gain my composure and hold her hand. She waits for her mother to get it together. The fireplace is raging while food sends a delicious aroma throughout the house, I am finally ready to speak when out of my bedroom pads a toddler with no name.

Dana Bea loses her cool and exclaims, "Mother!"

I calmly stand up with a heaving chest, blow my nose and say, "Yes dear, it's been a long winter."

Dana Bea decides not to scare the child and not to speak of subjects the little one might understand, so she coyly and sweetly asks the toddler, "Is that your dolly?" Then flashing me an awkward, forced smile, "I used to have a Raggedy Ann just like that."

I laugh out loud like a crazy person seeing my daughter's reactions, aware I have been caught red-handed. Coolly I add "Well if you like her dolly, you're going to really love her blankie."

Our dinner is delicious; we watch the little one happily eat while sitting at the table with three pillows under her rump and a small bath hand towel tied around her neck as a bib. Well, isn't this an interesting evening. We trot into the bathroom. I help her with her bath, then Dana Bea reads a story to her, and another, while I clean up the kitchen. As usual, we rock until she sleeps, and again, she is placed in my warm bed.

Later, after we have come back together as two adults and not day care providers, my daughter and I curl up on the couch, we toss a blanket over us. She has a million questions, and so do I. I jump in ahead of her, and don't wait to be polite. I spit out, "Dana Bea, seriously honey …"

"Oh great, when you address me as honey I know you want me to do something for you."

I continue on, "I need help, serious help" and spout out a list that has been rattling around inside my head. "I need a car seat, highchair, clothes, kiddie cups, diapers, you name it, I need it." I can't go anywhere to shop or run errands, and if you get my drift, nor can I leave her with anyone.

Dana Bea looks at me, then towards my bedroom door that houses a sleeping toddler with no name, looks back at me and says, "Oh yes, I do get your drift, I certainly do Mother, loud and clear."

Point blank she asks, "What are you doing about diapers Mother?"

I blurt out, "You need to buy the new type Dear, you know, the disposal kind."

"Tell me you are not using cloth."

"Well, I have cut up some double bed sheets, which I never use …"

"Okay Mother, go on …"

"… and terry cloth towels, kitchen towels too. I found two long diaper pins in the bottom of your cedar chest, and another one by chance on one of your dolls, thank goodness for that. It's been a very, shall I say, primitive journey … oh no … the throw-away diapers may seem odd to the garbage service …"

This small child with no name hears us, slips off the bed and toddles into the living room. My daughter and I chime in together in sweet

CHAPTER THREE

nonthreatening voices, "And look who just woke up. Okay, let's adjourn this meeting and talk about this after a good night's sleep." Dana Bea slips into the guest room, looks back at me, shakes her head, and softly shuts the guest room door.

Morning sun comes over the mountain and the toddler, the girl with no name, holds up Dana Bea's treasured childhood pink elephant.

"Oh yes, very sweet, may I hold your little friend?" Dana Bea asks. Again she flashes me a *Mother, why don't you give her everything from my childhood* look.

We have a fitful day, many details to work out and many hoops to jump through but mostly we tend to the child. Later in the day, after dinner; it's time for a bath then a few good books. Hopefully this will make us *all* sleepy. I rock her to sleep, and together Dana Bea and I put her to bed.

We again prepare to have an adult evening, while *you-know-who* sleeps. Dana Bea grabs my hand and leads me like a hostage towards the living room, to the couch where she has poured two glasses of red wine. We sit … smile … then she turns to me and directly asks, "Are you delusional?"

For some reason I bust out laughing and grunt out, "Yes, it seems I am."

She takes a sip, combined with a long thoughtful swallow and whispers, "Holy crap, Mom!"

We sit and stare at the fire.

Dana Bea sits down her glass of wine, and cradles her face in her hands, silent, thinking. I sit and wait for a lecture. And here it comes.

SECLUSION

My lovely daughter asks, "How did this happen, what is your plan … what are you doing … you didn't see this story on a soap opera did you … you are not going mental on me, are you?"

I lay my head back onto the couch and take a deep breath, stretch my legs and cross my ankles, look over towards my beautiful daughter and answer. "Yes, dear one, I am sane, healthy, happy and rich." I go on, "I have saved this small child from a life of abuse, verbal and physical and perhaps sexual assaults as well, with pictures to prove it. This is what I need from you daughter dear; I desperately need a fake birth certificate … I also need paperwork stating I am her legal guardian … I also need to get her into a doctor for her well baby checkup … I must have this paperwork … she needs a name, and a date of birth. I have to know her birth date to see a pediatrician. How old do you think she is?"

Dana Bea gulps the last of her red wine and belts out, "Is that all, are you sure?" then adds, "Let me get this list straight, you want me to get a counterfeit a birth certificate, and make up a date of birth, correct? Anything else, or do I have enough illegal requests?"

I explain, "A visit to a clinic or office will be highly suspicious if I don't know whether or not she has had her shots, and exams, I have no idea how old she is, plus dear, the doctor will see her scars."

Surprised, Dana Bea exclaims, "What scars?"

I take her hand, pull her off the couch and lead her back into the bedroom. The little one is fast asleep so I turn on the small lamp next to the bed and gently pull up her nightie. Very carefully I undo her diaper to expose her life of torture. Dana Bea gasps and has the same nauseating response as I had when I first witnessed this cruelty.

CHAPTER THREE

Later in the evening she asks, "What does she call you?"

"She calls me Nettie."

Dana Bea tries with all her might not to smile and repeats, "Nettie?"

"Yes, I am her safety net … I'm Nettie, and don't laugh."

Then she asks, "What are you going to name her?"

I confess, "I have no idea, something current, not too crazy, a name that will give her pride and a name to give her confidence. I am going to move to another town and raise her until I am caught and arrested and tossed in the slammer!"

Dana Bea's mouth drops open, "Mother!"

"Please help me … No don't help; you will be an accessory. Just give me advice and I will do whatever you come up with. No don't … don't get involved. I am so confused. What should I do next?"

Dana Bea looks at me with concern and asks point blank, "Do you think he suspects you, do you think he is watching you, or waiting behind that clump of pines on the corner, what is his deal anyway, and where is this toddler's mother? This situation is as abnormal as it gets; this is a very dangerous situation. You must pull yourself together. You are involved in something very serious, Mom. You have had her for how long now?"

I answer sheepishly, "Six weeks."

"Please be extremely careful Mom."

"Dana Bea; you go to the store with a list. No, second thought, I'll go to the store so you won't be involved; you stay home with the child. Tomorrow over coffee and breakfast we will write a list of needs and also look for a safe place for us to move; a relocation of sorts … No, tonight we'll write out the list. Yes, and relocate."

"Now Mom, I mean *Nettie,* calm down, tomorrow is a big day, yes I will help you, no worries and sweet dreams." Dana Bea now seems to be both intrigued and appalled at the same time.

Dana Bea sits at the breakfast table still dumbfounded. "You are not the same quiet Mother I used to know. Where did this passion come from?"

I smile and tell her to please deal with it, "Now please help me with the list, then when I return home, go skiing."

She chokes on her coffee and tries not to spit it out, then regains control and repeats, "Go skiing!" She belts out a laugh, "Are you nuts?"

She sits, sipping coffee while her lips rest on the rim of the coffee cup. With a hint of a smile, she pulls her head backwards and lets out a good strong laugh. "Okay Sergeant, here we go."

I continue to ramble on as I wash some dishes and stare out the window. "Dear, while you're at it, let's figure out a name, and will you please look at her teeth. See if you can tell her age by how many teeth she has, and where they are located; this will help us to zero in on her age … Okay Dear?"

CHAPTER FOUR

Professional Kidnappers

A few days zoom by, and still no name, but my daughter and I are getting more organized and nearly ready to launch the plan we have concocted. We have our supply list fulfilled and we also have a pantry and refrigerator full of foods and milk. I take a deep breath, pick up this sweet child and we rock, while Dana Bea prepares dinner, and with a giggle she says, "I'll ski tomorrow."

We are feeling very confident and secure with our plan, as topsy-turvy as it seems. Dana Bea mixes us a hot toddy and we sit back to relax and dive into some crumble cake. Then out of the quiet bedroom we hear the squeak of the bedroom door, the sounds of the rocker creaking and the fire crackling in the wood burning stove. We hear padding on the hardwood floors coming our way, and we are astonished to hear her soft voice say, "Nettie Dane."

She smiles and buries her shy face into her blanket. "See what I mean, there is no choice."

CHAPTER FOUR

Too quickly, our time together comes to an end. At the end of the week my daughter returns back to her home. I hate to see her go. I am trying so hard to be smart, and clever but I am full of turmoil, fear and hatred for those misfits, who by some freak of nature became parents. Dana Bea has a list of everything we need to do and vows to help. She wants to stay and continue this journey, this situation, this madness, but she is making her own life elsewhere, which is a smart thing to do while I dodge jail time.

We name her Jessica Rose, Jessica is a current popular name, and Rose because she is like a little rose I found in my winter garden. Dana Bea reads a few books on babies and surmises she is approximately two years old. She is dwarfed in her social skills and her small mechanical skills are not that of a two-year-old. She only wants to be rocked like a baby, and I'm fine with that. Whatever it takes for her to find her self-worth, her confidence and her ability to express herself and her emotions, is all fine with me.

I phone my daughter and state, "It's time to establish her birthday." Let's do the math." We both begin to talk about her size and teeth and speech. I recount when I found her in winter, right after New Year's Eve. "I noticed then that she was stalled emotionally, not faring well, and not progressing as she should, so let's give her at least a month from when she was probably born. Let's set her birthday at December 9, 1982; right between Thanksgiving and Christmas."

Our last name is Lane. My daughter and I say it together, Jessica Rose Lane. Okay, this is what we'll put on her fake ID and birth records, from this day forward. We can't believe what just came out of our mouths.

PROFESSIONAL KIDNAPPERS

Dana Bea phones late one night, unable to sleep she blurts out, "Where are her parents? If the doctor asks, you have to know where they are and why she is in your care. You can't say they are in prison because he can easily check. Say they are out of the country. No, they would need passports. You need to simply say, "They just took off."

"Mom, you must know why she has scars on her body. Don't go to a doctor until these answers roll off your tongue. Love you." And she quickly hangs up. I am so pleased to have someone jumping in to help, to step in and rescue me. She is in a better position to see beyond the bumps in the road and the downfalls. Now I fantasize that this situation is not so far out in left field and hopeful it just might work. Naturally I feel horrible that my daughter is awake all night thinking of the best ways to kidnap a child.

Dana Bea sent a certified letter. I sign the receipt, and open it to see a birth certificate for Jessica Rose. It has the raised seal from the state and feels real. It has the birth date we agreed upon, December 9, 1982. All the paperwork seems in order. Along with her birth certificate is the paper declaring I am Jessica's legal guardian. I fear to ask Dana Bea how she went about getting these fake documents. I ask her how much money she had to pay. But she is stubborn and has no indication of revealing her source nor the cost.

I prepare myself with answers and promise not to change up my story. If I do, this could trigger a huge red flag. Over and over I practice the answers so they will roll off my tongue.

My palms are sweating, I feel jumpy, nervous and faint as I place Jessica in her car seat safely hidden by the dark tinted windows of my luxury sedan. I drive to the doctor's office. I had located a clinic in

CHAPTER FOUR

another town, a larger town to help us blend in, and hopefully this day will be a very busy day so we will be pushed along and get what we need without too much fuss or suspicion. While standing at the desk I fill out the paperwork, and with shaking hands put down my address as the post office number I'd rented in town just a few days before. Then sit back down and wait with Jessica. I sit on my hands so they will stop shaking.

Jessica could be my granddaughter, or niece, or maybe a relative. We resemble each other and she looks a little bit like Dana Bea did as a child.

Sitting and waiting at this clinic is making me very nervous. I am so fearful of being exposed and arrested. But continue to sit and watch the clock, and begin to think back and remember when I found Jessica, her curly hair was camouflaged with filth and grit. It was a dirty mess with clumps of dried blood mingled in with some flannel. I quickly combed out the debris, and washed her hair, ending with a lavender conditioner to help with tangles. I feel she is too traumatized to have her hair trimmed, so it is rather busy and out of control. To help tame the curls Dana Bea bought her a couple of cute knit hats with little flowers on them.

I also have curly hair and as the years go by it is showing a few sprinkles of gray. I definitely look like her grandma, or someone's grandma. I feel thankful we resemble one another. Jessica has blue eyes, and round cheeks. She is very pretty and she has gained a fair amount of spunk, but she never disobeys or yells. Her inner person has already been squelched. In time, I believe she will find her voice and become her true self.

"How dare he beat this child, his child, or is he the father?" The longer time goes by, the more I want to hit this man over the head with a shovel.

PROFESSIONAL KIDNAPPERS

It has been an hour since we arrived, I hand Jessica some crackers and water, and we continue to wait.

Finally, the nurse comes to the door and calls, "Jessica."

I almost faint. I might be going to jail very soon, because I am a kidnapper, a liar and a very untrustworthy person. My heart beats with every step as I cross the room; just like in the story, *Tell Tale Heart* by Edgar Allen Poe. Jessica holds my hand, a kidnapper's hand and together we step through the well-used white door that leads us to the examination room.

Jessica sits on the examining table, I look at her and smile, but this scene is the worse, and the longest wait of my life, a convict's life. I talk to Jessica who seems happy and light hearted. I try not to give off an appearance of any wrong doing or inner demons. Knowing the truth, and living this lie is more than my brain can handle. Finally, the doctor enters the room. He is short, stalky and balding. He is cheerful and seems to know his business, which is unnerving.

He picks up her chart, looks at her fake birth certificate, with fake name and birth date. He reads longer than he should, looks up at me and asks, "Are you her grandmother?"

I casually lie, "Yes, I am."

He steps to the examining table and begins to feel her throat and under her arms, then puts on his stethoscope and lifts up her shirt. He listens to her chest, then gently lifts up her little pink floral shirt in the back and takes a long evaluation. He frowns and concentrates on her back and looks closely at her scars, rubbing his hands softly

CHAPTER FOUR

across the wounds. He puts his equipment away and looks straight at me. I innocently stare back. He asks me, "How did she get these?" I tell him the truth, the truth as my daughter and I had made up. I explain that her mother left town with her boyfriend a few months ago. He was abusive and they both use drugs. I stepped in, took over and am raising my granddaughter. "As you can plainly see this is a rescue."

He buys it. He looks at me again, his way is matter of fact as he tells me I am very brave, and my actions are commendable. He goes on and states the obvious, "She is very small for a two-year-old."

I agree and think to myself, oh, maybe her birthday should have been March 25 the following year, 1983. Maybe she is only one and a half. He suggests I return in three months for a follow up exam and he tells me to contact him if her mother and boyfriend are back in town. He stresses to keep her out of harm's way. I whole heartedly agree and get caught up in the lie, as if this is my real daughter we speak of; who runs with a man lower than dirt. Then I realize this lie, this assumption, makes me scummy by association. I listen, keep quiet and pray he does not phone the police after we leave.

Jessica sits patiently as he performs the rest of the exam. Then he asks me to hold her, while he gives her a pink liquid to swallow. Jessica smacks and licks her lips, seems pleased with this medicine, then he quickly gives her a shot in her thigh. Jessica cries out then begins to whimper, I hold her close and pat her back. He studies me, so conservative and meek. He must be wondering how I raised a girl like her mother. I so much want to tell him the truth, but instead I bite my lip and stay true to my kidnapper code of silence.

PROFESSIONAL KIDNAPPERS

Jessie and I continue to live imprisoned in my home, and our daily life consists of fairy tales, toys, home cooked meals, playtime, rocking time, nap time and warm bubble bath time. I chase her around in circles, and we sing together. I have taught her a few songs, and she has a little drum to hit. She is never far from her soft pink elephant. She is gaining weight as well as confidence and trust. One thing I do find odd is that she never looks out the window, she never peeks or asks to go outside. I know she needs to play with other children and learn social skills, but she doesn't seem ready.

Happily, she is now potty-trained, and boy do we celebrate. Smiles, hugs and much applause comes with each movement.

I watch her and evaluate her progress many times during the week. She is learning numbers, speaks clearly and her large and small motor skills are developing. She seems very content. She obviously needs this time to heal inside and out.

CHAPTER FIVE

Exposed

TWO MORE YEARS PASS and there is still no notice or mention of a missing toddler, it's as if she never existed. I get a glimpse of her mother, a word I use very generously. She has blonde hair with dark roots, it looks to be stringy and dirty. She is as skinny as a stick. I spot her when I drive by on my way home from the store. Confident with my tinted windows this has become a habit I have become addicted to for the past two years; driving by this rundown house with evil strangers lurking inside and out. There she is, Jessica's mother. She leans on the post by the patio, with a beer in her hand and a cigarette in the other. She looks much older than I expected. I have to wonder if she physically aged, and went downhill after her daughter vanished. I feel a twinge of guilt and sorrow for her as I slowly cruise by gawking at this woman who is too lazy or too weak to take a stand on right and wrong, to look for her daughter. Jessica at least deserved a search party.

I decide never to drive on their road again, a road appropriately named Shady Lane. I make arrangements to move to another town. Dana Bea came up for a few weeks to help. She has newspapers from

CHAPTER FIVE

many surrounding towns close to her work. I had already begun to pack and discard many items I have had most of my life.

I have to admit to myself that Jessica is probably one of those babies born with issues, due to the mother using drugs while pregnant. There is evidence in her motor skills and speech. I say nothing, but continue to observe and feed her nutritious foods and work with toys I order through the mail to stimulate her learning process.

She is almost four years old now, and has seen very few people. I take her to the grocery store in the very early morning hours, or to a park south of town. This park is where she meets other little children and they play together on the slides and swings. She and I play in my fenced backyard where we work on her motor skills and speech. Indoor time is playing with blocks and art, and hand-eye coordination. Jessica loves her easel, and she has produced masterpieces, which adorn my walls.

I have thought of moving to the East Coast, North Virginia, or the Florida Keys. Sometimes the thrill of living in Santa Fe passes through my mind, the rich culture fills my imagination. Finally, I realize I need to live close to my daughter, who is a fountain of strength.

Off we go on a road trip to the central California coast. I find many quaint bungalows in several nice towns. But this is a serious move, and I need to be sure. I reserve and pay for a storage unit just in case I need to move quickly.

I trade in my car and buy newer model in a different color with tinted windows. I keep it in the garage at all times and only go out to buy groceries or venture out to another town in search of playgrounds and parks. We live in seclusion, but she and I have an abundance of art supplies, music, dancing, and reading. She makes her own snacks, which is usually something frosted with sprinkles galore.

Watching her play one day I decide to take a break from packing and our life of secrecy. Today we will step out into the world. I take Jessica to her first county fair.

She has no idea what to expect; the excitement, the bright lights, the screams and the sounds she will hear as we enter the fairgrounds with all the rides and aromatic foods. I push her in her stroller, even though she is old enough to walk. The smell of straw and the different animal sounds guide us from one extreme fantasy of animals to another. We walk towards the huge barn and she wants out of the stroller. Hand in hand, we take a trip into a real barn to investigate the stalls. With smashed straw under our feet, we smell the animals, hear the animals and pet what we can, we wander through the maze of country life and into a world of farm animals she has only read about or seen on television. Her eyes are big, and full of wonderment. We walk along through the path and stop to look at many pens full of young groomed horses. She is in glorious heaven. We peek under rails to touch the soft curls of the sheep's wool, and laugh at the squealing piglets, while she holds her nose. She sees Shetland ponies and cows, and many other freshly groomed animals. She stares up at the size of a horse in wonderment, and the owner lets her pet the horse's nose. We avoid the rides, maybe next year. I explain to her about all the other fairs in the world. We'll try a different town one day I promise; planting the seed to move. She is tired and jumps back into her stroller.

We go to a trailer and look at the different foods, then we go into the building with homemade desserts and art. I buy homemade cookies

CHAPTER FIVE

and a glass of chocolate milk from a booth and continue to push her under the last warmth of the sun as it begins to set. She wants out again so she can look at all of the pies and cakes. I pull out a wet washcloth from my plastic bag and clean her up so we can move to the ostrich races and horse show. She jumps back into the luxury of her stroller.

To reach the entrance to the arena from the foods and art building, we have to walk past the beer booth which is located between us and the arena ticket sales booth. Lazily we move along, maneuvering between all sorts of people, when yelling and cussing penetrates the air and becomes louder and clearer. Shouts ring in my ears. I recognize the voice and instantly become fear struck. We head straight forward. Walking a tightrope; I dare not look either way. He is fighting, cursing and yelling with a group of men. Jessica puts her blanket over her head. Out of the corner of my eye I see a figure rushing towards us, pushing crowds aside as he closes in. He staggers right up to me, stops in my path and stares right into my eyes. He takes great pleasure to mock me in front of the gathering crowd. Seems he is angry and insults me for being out in public. This drunk is totally invested in me and my comings and goings. Inside I have to smile when I realize he is too drunk to notice, and totally misses the stroller with a child who sits inside, a four-year-old who sits inches away, his child. He leers at me, he is stumbling drunk and his beer breath clouds my face. Out of the crowd rushes a force who marches toward us. It is the skinny woman who is more than likely Jessica's mother. She yells and spouts off profanities to him and orders him to come back. She grabs his arms and drags him away. She does not give us a second glance. She smells of beer and stands within arm's reach of her missing daughter. My mouth is dry; a crowd gathers.

I feel a rage in me that wants to grab her by the neck, turn her face towards the stroller, and tell her, "See her, look at her face, this beautiful child is your daughter, you nincompoop."

But instead I watch them as they stumble, and sway back to their home away from home, the beer booth. He takes one more look back at me and notices the stroller. He fights like a gorilla to get away from his drunken buddies who overtake him and hold him down. He is on the ground with his friends sitting on his backside, too drunk to form a cohesive sentence and tell them why he is struggling. His pals are on him and subdue his rage. Jessica still has her head buried into her security blanket as I push her quickly into the arena and try not to alarm her, which is of course too late. I can't figure out why he is so angry with me, unless he recognizes me from living around the corner, and from the walk I took one night with Dana Bea. He must know I have his daughter. He knows, or strongly suspects, and hates me.

We look at the horses as promised for about one minute, and all the while I scan for an exit to get us out of the arena. I tell her the horses are sleepy and we have to let them get some rest. I look back, over to the left, and around the interior of the arena for an easy quick escape. My steps turn into a dead run, towards the exit sign, off to the right. Once out, I run past the booths, and horse stalls located at the back of the fair. I push past the crowd of gawkers and turn towards the large buildings full of handmade goods, quilts and pies. I turn and mix in with the large crowd and leave undetected.

In the distance I can hear him screaming loudly at the top of his lungs, "Snotty bitch!"

I turn and run, pushing Jessica along the way, and head out the double gates to the safety of my car. I put Jessica in the seat next to me, fold

CHAPTER FIVE

up the stroller, toss it into the backseat and jump in, no seatbelts. I pull over to a gas station two blocks away and secure her in her car seat. I drive out of town for close to twenty-five miles until I find a motel with a lit vacancy sign. This is where we spend the night, hiding from a mad man. She asks no questions even though we ran through the crowd, darting and dashing along the paths in a frantic run though the fair, then in between hundreds of parked cars.

I phone my daughter, and she makes arrangements to meet us at the motel the next day. She drives most of the night to help us. The next morning, I hire a moving company who will meet us at my house to help pack. I urge them to work quickly and promise to give them a nice sum of cash once we arrive at my new home. The movers will arrive at my house by 11:00 A.M.

Auntie Dana Bea arrives at the motel the next morning and gathers up little Jessica. Dana Bea had stopped by my house to pack a bag for Jessica. She filled it with a few stuffed toys, clothes, and jammies. Thank heavens Jessica is exhausted from yesterday's adventure at the fair. She is curled up with her blanket and lets us women fuss and run around in circles. Dana Bea takes the stroller which carries her favorite blanket with her pink elephant tucked inside the flap on the back side of the stroller. I hug Dana Bea real tight, then Jessica, who thinks it's another adventure with her Auntie, hugs me back, but seems clueless that we are moving.

Dana Bea drives them to a café where they have an early lunch and she has a huge coffee drink and one to go. Then she begins the long drive back to her home in San Luis Obispo.

I stay behind to meet the movers and continue to pack. Two of the burly movers help me throughout the day. It is amazing what extra cash can provide; *protection*. I feel safe and strong, so I concentrate on packing up my life. I am also frantic inside, but determined to vanish.

Everything I am made of wants to dial the police, and turn in this fool for abuse, torture and possible molestation, plus years of being drunk and disorderly in public. This is not a good idea for many obvious reasons; I might end up sharing a cell with him. I want to phone his landlord to alert this poor guy about the condition of his home, but I have no idea who he is and I have to remind myself that my days of snooping are finished. I am leaving this crazy life behind.

I phone a realtor and ask her to stop by the house today, tomorrow will be too late. She looks around and we agree on a price. I mention she needs to hire a cleaning lady as I am leaving the next morning. I give her my Post Office box address and Dana Bea's phone number.

Outside in the backyard, I have to take a deep breath and realize that I must leave and never look back. I say goodbye to my home and to my lovable dog Buddy, who is buried over there under the Lilac bush that adorns the corner of my backyard, it sits right next to the rock water feature, the lilac is sporting its spring growth of flowers and I so hate to give it up. I ask Jim to stay with me and explain to him that I am doing what life has handed me and to please help me, please guide me if he is able. "Jim, please ask for a day pass and help me."

Under the stars I vow to forget this monster and continue on with my life, a life with Jessica, a life I am proud of and a life well lived. I say a dramatic goodbye to my backyard and Buddy, this gives me a sense of security and purpose, with a smidgen of closure.

CHAPTER FIVE

Side by side, the big guys continue to pack and tape boxes. They write the contents on each box, which sometimes is a question mark. I tell them, if we can't pack it, it stays, they nod and give off a smug smile, as they know I am on the verge of hysterics. The packers are professionals and everything goes, they overlook my demands as I pack Jim's tools, his files, our personal papers, my files and all medical records on Jessica. I am diligent to pack her toys, blankets, and clothes, and artwork, to make sure all hints of a child on the premises are removed. I never close my eyes to catch a wink of sleep, not once. I keep packing. The truck pulls up on time at 8:00 A.M. The two men begin to fill the truck, never asking any questions. I fill my car with food, personal items and anything I might need in case I have an emergency, then add a thermos of black coffee.

I know my girls are waking up in another town, and this brings a sense of relief as I continue to collect and toss my kitchen wares into a box with beans, canned beets, soups and cook books.

The men put the last of the boxes in a pile and continue to organize and pack the truck. Across town I arrive at the bank and withdraw all my money, close my account and walk away with a check and some cash for the movers. We have arranged to meet at the weigh station so I can follow them south.

Just before the truck arrives I call Dana Bea who quickly spits out her achievements; she and Jessie are fine and she has secured a place for us to live. It is a long story she adds, something about an old friend is all she has time to say.

"Hope you like it. See you soon." She quickly gives me the address for the movers. She adds, "We can deal with your storage unit later."

EXPOSED

The reality of not seeing my next home is somewhat daunting, but I trust her judgement, and we need a roof over our heads. The irony of this is overwhelming with a glint of surprise. The speed of this move and the art of fleeing excites me. This once organized, boring person who never made a fuss in her life, is haphazardly tossing her life into boxes and moving to an unseen, unknown location with a child she has kidnapped. I see this as the ticker tape that will run across the bottom of the television set all over our country and maybe beyond. Right then and there, the second this thought dashes across my brain I truly decide to go for it. To run and hide, and evaporate into thin air. No mistakes and no second guessing.

The drive south is very time consuming, with winding roads and repetitive landscape. I follow the truck for hours, and chew on an apple I had tossed in the front seat, next to a bottle of water, and still we drive. I sip coffee all the way. Our caravan crosses the Bay Bridge and meanders through the east side of larger cities. Now, we are truly heading south, I keep close contact with the truck, with my life on wheels.

Finally, we maneuver through the rolling hills, past small towns, winding through the redwoods until I finally sense the ocean. The truck pulls over at a fast food diner, and I follow along and park next to them. They go in to eat while I pull out a small iced lunch bag. I make a phone call to my daughter while chewing on a tuna sandwich. She knows exactly where we are and promises to meet us in one hour. I had no idea we would be this close to the ocean, I had wondered if my home would be up in the hills to the east, but Dana Bea's directions are clear.

The engines start up, the car and truck continue to caravan. The two burly men wave me on to lead the way.

CHAPTER FIVE

We continue to head in the direction of the ocean, and I wonder what my daughter has done. She loves to shake me up and thrives on surprising me, I suspect this will be her moment to shine.

We pull up to a very tiny beach town, and carefully drive down a road that follows along behind what looks like the main street. I see a boardwalk, a parking lot for the public and a private covered parking structure for residents. We slowly drive along, looking for an address as I follow her directions.

The truck stops, Dana Bea points to the bungalow and gives them the key and house number. I jump out to see my beautiful daughter and Jessica who stand there unsure what to do, then they both smile. Running hugs feel so good. They attack me with bear hugs and it feels so good. I take a few steps back and look up at a rocky hillside. It is mostly jagged rock formations with duplexes dotting the hillside.

I put my arm around her waist, pull her in tight and congratulate her with, "Good one Dana Bea."

Our new home sits high up at the very end of the steps, with a view of the beach, and a full view of the endless ocean. Dana Bea informs me she paid someone to clean just this morning, and then she emphasized, *deep clean*. The refrigerator she has stocked with food. It's tiny, a one bedroom with a smaller alcove, or den. Perfect. I swirl around and give her a big, long hug. We are safe, obscure and on top of the world. "I love you dear one." I whisper into her ear.

Dana Bea tells me her company gave her two days off to help with family matters.

"Family matters, ha! Now that is an understatement." I love her description of total chaos, painted in pastels with two simple words; *family matters.*

"Well Mother, it does sound better than the Kidnappers Relocation Project."

We give Jessie some open boxes so she can help; she drags out blankets and washcloths. She puts soap in the bathtub and stays busy. We unpack each box, and it is just like Christmas. We have to laugh. It looks as if Jessica had packed for us. What a mish mash of goods and mismatched items: very little is labeled, and I don't care.

The sheets go on, and they are not the right size. Too big, which is better than too small, and I don't care about that either. Dana Bea and I quickly tuck in the oversized sheets that drag on the floor.

We continue to put the bungalow together, then stop and wonder why are we rushing, we look at each other thinking, "What's the rush?" We decide to take a break. The three of us step down the long staircase with a wooden rail that follows along the rocks to the beach and boardwalk. Many delicious foods are available and many tables and chairs line the edge next to the beach. Jessica begs to touch the sand. We pack up our food and sit on a bench with our feet in the sand. We watch her run in circles, drop to her knees and giggle.

Music plays in the background on the boardwalk, we hear the sounds of games, and bells when the ball hits its target. I love it, Yes, I truly love this place, the atmosphere is relaxed and easy going. This little beach town is alive. Instantly I enjoy the sounds from a song on the loud speaker. I ask Dana Bea if she knows who is playing this music. She smiles at my innocence and tells me it is a band called Journey. "Perfect name for a band playing for us," I tell her.

We bump our paper cups together, then happily toast to our journey. Jessie enjoys playing in the sand while we lean our heads back and lap up the warmth of the sun.

Dana Bea looks over towards me and smiles, "I don't know who you are these days, it sure is a rapid, crazy life."

Dana Bea confides how proud she is of me for not letting Jessica slip into the system. "Your idea sprouted from shock and fear, then slid into love, you are doing a very powerful thing, just keep your eyes and ears on alert and never, never let up. You will always be breaking the law Mom. Don't trust anyone."

We click our cups together again and watch a little four-year-old run across the sand, slide and squeal.

CHAPTER SIX

Living a Lie

SPRINGTIME IS THE BEACON FOR TOURISTS to venture out to the beach. In my mind I think, Jessica should start Kindergarten this fall, but I feel a dark cloud over me when I consider this. Meditation helps to clear my troubled mind about this day, and exposure. With deep thought, and consideration I decide to look for someone to home school her. I am thankful we have a few spring months left, and the summer to acclimate and establish ourselves as a normal family.

Our complex is filled with singles, divorcees, small children and some very private couples. Jessie spends her days with me. I love to watch her play on the beach with the other local kids. Now and then they come to our house for snacks. I love to see the kids run up the long never ending staircase, with such energy and joy in everything they do.

I teach Jessica to spell, speak well, and together we work on her vocabulary. She helps clean up in the kitchen, and happily stands on her newly painted pink stepping stool to do the dishes.

CHAPTER SIX

Still consumed with finding a teacher to home school her, I stew and fret about Jessica's fake birth certificate, and the idea it will not pass inspection if the home teacher asks for one. Considering a private school, I pray she will meet more girls her age, and not just the few who live close by. Private schools are credited, there will be a paper trail—but maybe not as obvious as public schools.

The stove temperature is ready and I stir the warm play dough, a favorite childhood craft she loves. Dana Bea and Jessica spend a lot of time squishing play dough into the shapes of animals or peeling off images from the newspaper.

I apply Aloe Vera to her scars to help them minimize and heal. They seem to be healing as well as her memory of abuse.

In the local paper is an announcement of a private K–8 school opening. On Monday I take her with me for an interview. The school is called Steps. It is privately funded and works on donations and payments per class. I sign Jessica up for Kindergarten and hope this new school takes wing and flies.

The teacher and I talk while Jessie plays with toys, stares into the aquarium to watch the turtle, then onto the next one which is full of tropical fish. Sure enough, teacher Sandy asks if I am Jessica's grandmother. I lie as usual, and try to keep my story the same; still repulsed to be identified as the mother who raised Jessica's loser mother. I inform teacher Sandy that Jessica calls me Nettie. I go on and tell her that Jessica's mother is away on a trip, and use the word *trip* very loosely.

I pay the tuition fee and the teacher, Miss Sandy lets Jessica pick out her own cubby, then Miss Sandy puts Jessica's name on it, across the top. School will begin in three weeks, and we are both overjoyed.

LIVING A LIE

In a blink of an eye the first day of school arrives. Jessica is scared. Her joy switches to reality. We walk into the classroom at 8:00 A.M. She keeps her little sweaty hand in mine, we stand there for a minute, then she lets go and carefully hangs up her sweater in her cubby and checks to see if the turtle is still there. One by one other young children arrive. All the students are shy, some cry and cling to their mothers. Many come in with a grandparent. I watch and stay with Jessie for about ten minutes, kiss her cheek, and tell her I'll be back at noon. I point up to the clock above the door and show her the twelve. She stays close to that turtle.

Steps is a Godsend. The teacher and her college student aids, who are interning to receive units from the local college, are eager beavers. Each day the cute college helpers are there for three hours. Happy, overly energetic and they speak in young voices.

We enjoy wintering through our window to the ocean. Thanksgiving is at Dana Bea's house, then two weeks later we celebrate Jessica's birthday. Steps also has a party for her special day. Then, Christmas is upon us. Steps goes all out with the children's Christmas artwork.

Steps resumes in January and Jessica is happy to reconnect with her classmates. Being a small beach town, you would think this school could not survive financially. The surprise is, many parents want to break away from the traditional educational program and let their children enjoy a nonconventional learning process. They commute from around the outlining area to attend Steps. This school encourages us to stay and watch our child, or help in the kitchen. But I quickly leave and avoid conversation with the other parents and grandparents.

CHAPTER SIX

The college student interns took the children on a field trip to the fire department. Each child got to climb up and sit behind the wheel of the big red fire truck. A fireman that one of the interns described as, "cute" showed the kids a tall brass pole and explained how the firemen slide down the pole, and jump into the truck.

School comes to an end and it's time for summer play. Steps stays open year round for working parents, but you pay per day. We happily hit the beach with our buckets, scoopers and beach towels.

Lea, Jessie's friend from Steps comes over as much as she is allowed, which is nearly every day. Our front yard is the sandy beach, and the girls play all day, perfecting their cartwheels.

In August, we buy new clothes and a back pack and drive back to Steps. Jessica is a first grader, and still keeps a watchful eye on the turtle. This place is full of energy and action. I still feel nervous because I have no record of her life except the one Dana Bea and I made up. Dana Bea boasts and smiles when she recalls the day she found the unsavory guy who makes fake IDs, mostly so college kids can get into bars. She approaches this man who had been pointed out by a friend of a friend on campus. She gives him some sort of a cock and bull story about a fire and the loss of important papers. He doesn't care, he is clearly a criminal and tells her he just wants the money to begin, and the rest of the cash after the documents are complete. He brags that the paperwork will also have the raised stamp, like the real seal from the state. "It looks and feels real." He brags.

LIVING A LIE

I miss Jessie after having her home all day throughout the summer months. I don't know what to do with my free time, where to begin. I busy myself cleaning and being the housewife I was trained to be. Then, before you know it it's time to walk down the long stairs, drive to the school and retrieve my little student. There she sits, on the window seat with her best friend Lea.

This year, fall is short lived. The ocean is more aggressive, with an endless show of impressive high waves that crash down on the shore and rocks. There are fewer tourists at this time of year, and our small town becomes family. While the wind whips up the sand Jessie and I tend to ourselves and stand inside at our bay window to watch nature at its finest.

She celebrates another birthday, and another Christmas.

Parents these days don't drive their kids to school every day; a few of us from the area have started up a car pool. All is ideal and Jessie is very happy and secure. Walking down the long steps to the parking lot is a daily experience of balance and bravery. She jumps into the waiting car with her friends and off they go. She also enjoys being in my taxi picking up each friend.

Second grade zooms by and the quiet couple next door to us is moving. My heart pounds at the thought of who might move in, who might know us. No children move out, so Jessie is none the wiser with the change of neighbors.

Returning home from dropping Jessie off at Lea's house for a celebration party I notice a moving truck backed up to the bottom of the

CHAPTER SIX

stairs and boxes in the arms of big guys who walk carefully and weave their way up the staircase. I keep my head down, and slip into my duplex, to escape into my secret nest.

I see and hear nothing. A ghost has moved in next to me.

Daily I cruise by the neighboring deck. I have learned each step without looking, Jessie and I both trot smoothly and quickly up or down. Feeling brave as time goes by, school is out and each day becomes one vacation day after another.

One day on my way up the steps, with my arms full of groceries, I notice a lawn chair in front of the once empty duplex, it sits on the small wooden patio we each have. There is also a small table next to the chair. I slither past and keep my eyes on my toes.

I never smell food next door; never hear a sound. Who is there? Are they watching us? I ask my daughter to come over this weekend to see if she can get a sighting or a feel, if anything is wrong. I ask her to help me pay attention to details next door. We walk to the storage sheds and their unit is locked. I see no car and have to wonder why. Are they undercover agents or is it a private investigator searching for this child, I fret. I am as paranoid as a nice lady can be.

Dana Bea sees nothing and regrets she is unable to give me any advice or offer any magical insight. We walk along the shore, talk, look up towards the balcony and see nothing on our decks.

"Mom, they, he or she might be very nice, maybe quiet, or newlyweds, or a very private person, or a scared lady like yourself." I look at her with worry across my brow, the sun in my face and say nothing, and still there is no movement and no signs of life, day after day.

The only sign of life next door is the curtains opening and closing. This will be an interesting summer. I find it difficult to be invisible and conquer this lifestyle. I will focus, try to be pleasant and act as if nothing is out of order.

Jessica is a dream. She is quiet, patient and loves me unconditionally. She has new friends and bounces around ready to visit at a friend's house, or meet them on the warm sandy beach below our duplexes. We must stay with a routine, yet be ready for trouble. Every so often I rub her back with Aloe Vera to help with the scars that resemble a road map across her backside. While outside on the beach, she usually wears a t-shirt over her bathing suit. We buy the racing style swimsuit, a one piece with a higher back. She tells me her best friend Lea asked her why she has scars on her back and legs. She adds, "I told her it was from a car accident or a fall, that I couldn't really remember." She innocently asks, "Nettie, will you tell me?"

"Honestly, yes honey, one day when you are a little bit older we will have a nice long talk." She listens. "One day I will tell you everything you want to know, but for now, you enjoy your friends, the beach and your young happy life."

She smiles and agrees. Jessica's clock is ticking, and one day I will have to face the truth, and tell her about her abuse and show her the file along with the photos.

CHAPTER SIX

In late May it happens; I meet my neighbor. I meet the mystery man who lives next door. Standing on my small private deck overlooking the rocks and beach I breathe in the amazing salt water air, and feel a presence behind me. I turn with a jerk and there he stands.

He smiles a crooked smile, then in a low southern drawl he introduces himself. "Hi, looks like I'm your neighbor, you can call me Sam. Sorry if I startled you."

I lean back to have more space between us and stare at this beautiful specimen of a human being. I am completely spell bound. This feeling makes me shudder, swallow hard, and finally spurt out, "Oh no, no, no you didn't surprise me. Well, yes you did actually."

All of my skills of speech from college and deliberate composure fly off the deck, and tumble down the rocks. Here I stand with the wind whipping my long black hair with gray streaks trying to makes some sense. It blows all over my face while I babble.

Sam is gigantic and has massive amounts of pure white hair. He is very tan and wears an old rayon Hawaiian shirt, worn comfortable shorts and flip flops. My light weight floral cotton dress touches the tops of my feet, and flows along with my hair. Out of nervousness, I pull it back into a ponytail and secure it at the base of my neck. The force of the wind causes my curls to escape.

I smile back while I internally and secretly dig deep for restraint and say, "Nice to meet you Sam." But I so want to blurt out, "So very nice to meet you *Mr. Tan Hands.*" This thought makes me smile from guilt, and reminds me I am a woman.

He smiles back with a sexy crooked smile and slowly states the obvious, "Well aren't you a silly one."

He must have read my mind and this is not going well. I cannot think of one thing to say, nor do I have any questions. He takes his extra-large tan hands and slides them along the sides of his hair to help control it during the wind dance. I beg for my knees to not buckle.

My inner common sense voice rescues me. "Come on now. He might be a detective, Don't let yourself be blindsided by his rugged sexy looks and his southern charm. Do not. Find your intelligence, your caution, your inner strength girl. For the love of God, snap out of it."

I offer him a slice of warm bread and coffee. He smiles and says in his low slow drawl, "Why thank you Mam, sounds delicious, I will certainly take you up on that offer."

I quickly tell him that I'll bring it out here on my patio. Jessica is at a friend's house as I serve a stranger, a possible FBI informant, brunch.

Our conversation is quite odd. He is smooth, casual, and confident while I struggle to be what I think he wants or what I wish I was, and while I fight to keep my guard up and select the correct answers. He chuckles and I laugh back. At this moment I know better than anyone how uncomfortable I am in my own skin.

The zucchini bread is a big hit and I can't help but notice how much he enjoys our visit. I choke out, "Thank you," and go on to say, "I always use more cinnamon than the recipe calls for, and a dash of ginger too, I

CHAPTER SIX

got the recipe from my cousin Fair." I hate it that I am so weird, tossing out needless information off the top of my head, but I can't stop myself. It pops out naturally, I smile and think to myself, *"It's a gift, really."*

He swallows his bread, takes a long slow sip of coffee and asks, "You have a cousin named Fair?" Then adds, "That surely is a southern name."

"Well yes, I do have some southern blood in my family." He smiles and continues to keep an eye on the ocean.

I decide to step up and be the woman I was when I kidnapped my gal Jessica. I ask him where he is from and how he happened to find this quaint place.

He looks over at me, with that crooked smile and slowly says, "Texas, and finding this place was pure luck."

"Oh, okay. Well then, it's too early for a glass of wine, ah, so I guess I better get the dishes clean and sweep the sand off the patio."

He stands up, I bend my head back and look up to see his face, and his million-dollar smile.

"No Missy, how's about you don't clean up and sweep just yet, how's about you grab your sandals and let's head to the beach and take a walk," he suggests.

Without a brain in my head, I bend over, slip on my sandals and walk ahead of him, down the long steps as ordered.

We hit the beach, he takes five steps and yells, "Come on."

He kicks off his sandals and keeps running. I bend down, kick off my sandals, pick up the bottom of my cotton dress, pull it up to my knees and take off running after him, running as I have never run before. Here I am, chasing a Texan along the surf.

We run together, stop, laugh and slowly walk along in the surf, we pick up shells, while I forget who I am. My entire life and all memory of my past life vanish, just flew out to sea with the seagulls. Sam walks over to me, smiles and picks me up in his arms and runs towards the ocean, jumping over white small bubbles from the tide and small waves.

Finally, when we are out in the water waist deep, he twirls me around and around and tosses me high up in the air. I tumble into the ocean and my cotton dress turns into a balloon and floats in the water. My hair hangs over my face so I blow it out of the way. He picks me up, grins, and without thought, I jump on his back and ride him like a horse. I think I even kick his hips a couple of times as he gallops us back to shore. We are laughing and having the best time when he slows down to a trot. He stops, and we reclaim our composure.

I look up at the sky, at all the fluffy clouds, then look towards the rocks and duplexes when I see her. There stands my daughter. She has been watching us from my patio, leaning on the rail with her arms folded; I reach out my arm and wave to her, and she returns with a small half friendly wave. He slips me off his back, I pick up my soaked dress and try to shake it so the sand will fall back onto the beach; just as any well-trained lady from the Long Branch Saloon would do.

Sam says, "You've got company."

CHAPTER SIX

I tell him, "Yes, that's my daughter, Dana Bea, I have always called her Dana Bea because she is my little honey."

He grabs my hand and says, well, let's go back up there so I can meet your Miss Dana Bea. Together we walk up the staircase to face reality. I call out, "Oh, hi honey."

She smiles back. "Well hello Mother."

"Hi honey, this is Sam." She smiles and we three stand and have an awkward moment of silence.

"Sam is my next door neighbor." I explain. Hoping she won't blow my cover as an overly cautious neighbor who suspects him to be the enemy, I hold my breath.

Without getting too close, she stretches out her long thin arm, leans forward and says, "Nice to meet you Sam."

Sam, without hesitation says, "Likewise."

Oh dear. I am caught red handed; being happy. I stand there on my patio, wet and sandy, while Dana Bea asks if she can fetch a towel. I answer quickly, and to my astonishment reply. "No honey, I think I'll let the wind and the sun dry my dress and hair."

She looks flabbergasted then turns to look at Sam who just stands there with that goofy smile and listens. Finally, I spit out, "Beautiful day."

She adds, "Yes, lovely."

LIVING A LIE

Sam smiles, "You have a very energetic mom."

Dana Bea smiles a forced grin then looks at me while I blush. She is obviously not as captivated by his charms as her mother. We are actors in a preteen pathetic scene, and I am out of my mind with excitement. He nods and takes three steps back into his home.

I look at my daughter who asks the obvious, "Where is Jessica?"

"She's at Lea's." I bluntly respond.

With a touch of urgency, my daughter makes a suggestion, "Mom, let's go inside, you take a shower while I get us something to eat."

I give her a huge hug and while looking over her shoulder say, "No honey, I think I'll just stand out here and enjoy the view, and the memory of what just happened and let my wet dress slowly dry out. You go ahead, there is plenty of food in the fridge." I release my hug, look at her face and smile.

She walks into my place, pours us some fresh ice water, sits down at the small round mosaic table and waits for me to sit down and come to my senses.

I gulp the water and ask if she will ride along with me to retrieve Jessica, she happily jumps to her feet. We lock up the house, I reach down, pull up my damp dress and jog down the steps to the car.

Alone and away from my rosy heart throb next door, and the fresh memory of the sand and sea, she turns to me and asks, "Mom, what was that all about?"

CHAPTER SIX

I realize she is now the mother and I the daughter. I have to laugh at this and sooth her imagination, "Nothing, really, just some long overdue flirting and innocent fun."

"Seriously mother, I watched you, you were riding him like a stallion." With this statement we both let out a whoop and a duet of loud boisterous laughs.

I sigh, "Oh my lord I did!" I gush, "Oh my dear, he came out of nowhere. He simply scooped me up into his arms. Do you realize, not once in my entire life has anyone carried me in their arms! He is as smooth as silk. I hope he is real, and not a plant by the FBI." I tell her with a sigh, "I pray we have another day at the beach."

Dana Bea listens to her out of control mother's schoolgirl crush, not realizing how lonely I have been all these years and innocently asks, "What does he do for a living mother, and what brings him to this part of the state, where is he from?"

I sheepishly look at her and answer, "I have no idea. I do need to have a nice long chat with him, but outside on the patio of course and I promise to be more lady like."

Dana Bea takes a deep breath, gathers her thoughts and continues to listen to her mother's sandy adventure.

CHAPTER SEVEN

Gracious Neighbor

"Mother, listen please, I've met someone. This is the reason I stopped by." Dana Bea smiles and tells me they met at a downtown business association meeting.

"He is two years older than me, and comes from Eugene Oregon." She excitedly goes on and describes how they think alike and have the same energy, "Mom, he is my mirror. He likes to hike, snow ski, travel and he loves to cook."

I question his motives because of Jessica, and know this is not fair to Dana Bea, but I have to ask. "Did he come up to you and introduce himself, or did you pursue him? Have you mentioned Jessica to him?"

Dana Bea smiles and says, "You are such a worry wart, seriously mother, I met a man I really care for, and for just once can we keep Jessie out of it."

CHAPTER SEVEN

Her mini lecture shakes me back to reality, now I understand the importance of her conversation and what it means to her. I apologize, "I'm sorry Dana Bea, out of fear I have turned your news back to my life of crime. But dear, naturally I'm leery of a relationship when it progresses too quickly."

Long pause … Dana Bea shocks me with her response, and returns my apology with a sharp response, "Well, isn't this the pot calling the kettle black!"

Sheepishly I smile back, "Okay you got me on that one, sorry."

"Honey, what is his name?"

She grins and answers, "Rex, but everyone calls him Coach." She then spills her heart.

Our once simple organized secret life is beginning to bulge with outsiders. This is how life should be, moving forward and multiplying not receding.

We pull up to a tidy house in a quiet neighborhood and Jessica runs towards us. I yell thank you to Lea's mom and wave goodbye. Simple, as it should be.

We decide to go out for pizza tonight and relax a bit. Jessica is so happy to be out in public, and she loves pizza. While she is eating and maneuvering melted cheese, my daughter and I look at each other and silently agree, we need to talk. We surmise we can't do this at my place (thin walls) and we can't talk in front of *you know who*, I wink when she looks up. Dana Bea points out the obvious, school is almost out and Jessica is home all summer, except for play dates with friends.

"Let's see, how about I phone you when our gal has another play date at a friend's house and we'll meet at a quiet coffee shop."

A week later we meet at Bottoms Up, talk and sip hot coffee. We brainstorm, connect and sort out details of her life and mine and our little one Jessie. Life is so great right now for both of us, let's hope it stays this way. I need to cool it with my neighbor until I know it is safe.

Jessie is in a good place, school is going well, and Dana Bea is already planning her wedding. Their engagement flew by in record speed. Coach didn't skip a beat after he met my girl Dana Bea. They set the date, deciding the best time for them to get married is after baseball season.

Many days, and weeks are spent jogging on the beach with my big Texan. When together, we have the time of our lives. He is so comfortable to be with, and I cherish our free time. I have no backbone to *cooling* down our relationship. Instead, I choose to enjoy the ride.

He and I continue to meet for morning coffee on my patio, take runs and talk. When Jessica is home from school or on weekends we include her in our runs and playfulness. We make sand castles with motes, and they threaten to bury me. We always have buckets and a scooper to take with us to the beach. Sometimes all you can hear are the waves and the patting of our hands as we create a village. Lea joins us sometimes, she and Jessie are a good match; they mesh together like sisters.

CHAPTER SEVEN

Time moves on, and summer flies by. Today we experience a long warm fun day on the beach. We walk home as the sun begins to set. Trudging back up the long steps, we finally arrive to our little duplex.

We are always sandy, with knees soiled, and look forward to a warm shower. Jessica is pooped out from too much fun. I tell her to take a bath before mine. Time to clean the house, and as always, sweep the sand outside, then get our supper dishes out of the way. Sam steps into his place and waves goodbye, with his cute grin. Jessica crawls into bed after a warm meal and falls sound asleep.

Today has been an exhausting day. I smile to myself, then softly step into a hot shower. Gently the sand slides off my body. I look down at my aging body to assess the inventory. Working my hands in a circular motion, I gently cover myself with bubbles made from lavender soap. Slowly and with care I cleanse my arms, legs, chest and neck. I toss shampoo into my thick hair and wash out the sand. This is the moment an image of my neighbor, a clear vision of him comes into my head, and I secretly day dream of a life together. My head tilts back and warm water flows through my graying hair and trickles down my back. I lift my head and watch the suds slowly move along my body and cascade over my breasts, I gently rub them. I look down at myself again and think, "I am too old to think these thoughts." The suds band together and slide down my body. I tell myself you are all used up, too busy, too tired, and too needed.

I reach down and turn the water off, step out of the tub, squeeze the water out of my hair, then wrap a towel around it, and begin to dry the water off my skin. I feel alive again, but in a different way. I like the way it feels, young and sensual. But my inner person, the one I have always battled with begins to pull me back to reality, whatever reality is; logic tells me to stop being silly. You are not a spring chicken, you are Nettie, you are a young girl's life, her rescuer. You are her grandmother.

With my hair still inside a towel, I slip on a silk Kimono, tying the sash nice and tight. In a few steps I look towards the window to gaze outside and stare at the ocean. There he sits.

I continue to enjoy the view, but dare not step outside, not one big toe. Why is he so visual lately, he wasn't when he first moved in next door? What is it about him that makes no sense? What is he hiding. I tilt my head to the side and squeeze the towel as I pull it off.

Sam looks over his right shoulder and sees me. He waves his hand like a child, with all fingers moving up and down at the same time, very endearing. I stand as if imbedded in concrete. I can't move, I dare not. I smile, reach forward and close the curtains.

Stewing on my couch, I wrestle with womanly intuition while fighting with my secret desires. I have to remember to be careful, very careful. "Think of Jessica's safety, the ramifications of being caught, foster care, and life in prison. Think."

Days pass, we avoid each other. He is in his place most of the time and I in mine. I bolt past his window on my way down the steps while holding hands with Jessie. She and I play on the beach, just the two of us, but now we are on the other side of the Boardwalk. This childish dance lasts into early autumn. I am afraid, he must feel it too.

Every now and then I hear a television or the sounds of someone preparing food. Once I thought I heard the sounds of him sweeping. He doesn't sit on his patio these days. The silence between us is deafening. This game

CHAPTER SEVEN

of not looking at each other is becoming awkward, more apparent, and uncomfortable.

One evening I hear a faint knock at the door. The kind of knock that doesn't want to wake a sleeping child. I wait, listen, then another tap, tap, tap. I stand up, take a few steps and open the door. There he stands.

Sam and I stay up most of the night talking. I ask him point blank questions and he answers. He asks me some very uncomfortable questions also. I skirt the issue of my grandchild Jessica and my life in the mountains in Northern California. We speak of our past, our childhoods, our siblings, our parents, our life in high school, and college, my marriage, his marriage, my daughter, his son. Then he speaks of the elephant in the room, my granddaughter Jessica.

I pretend not to hear this question and continue on. I dodge this topic faster than a slippery fish in a river. He pats my hand, then his hand slips off mine and rests on top of my thigh, which is covered by my kimono. I try to keep my cool while this exciting man touches my thigh with his outrageous sexy weathered hand. He continues to touch the silk, but never me, which is driving me to a new heightened emotion. I try my best to appear calm and unaware, and continue to jabber.

He says he is not a spy and he is not with the FBI nor is he a private detective. He notices, and it is apparent that I am spooked with strangers, and he assures me he likes his space, and he respects my privacy. Even though he is all over my silk robe, he says this with a straight face; he respects my privacy. This makes me smile behind my face, void of expression, I look down at his hand, then back up to his face.

He explains he is a former Texas Ranger from Houston Texas. With a pounding heart, I try to keep my fear in check. Worrying this a trap.

Sam tells me he has a friend, Hansen, his former partner, before they each retired. Hansen and his wife moved to this area to work in drilling for an oil company. Sam tells of following his friend out here to sunny California. He decided, "Why not."

Hansen and his wife Connie were very helpful. They found his duplex. The very day it went for rent on the open market, Hansen snatched it up. He explains he was having his clothes and property shipped out while his duplex was being cleaned and painted.

That is why the place was rented and no one was there. It all makes sense.

Sam says he likes the privacy and the ambiance of this place, and enjoys the view. I agree, but keep my cards close to my chest and don't reveal any extra information. I tell him about Jim, our life, and my life as a devoted wife. He learns the details of Jim dying in my arms and about the love I have for my daughter.

Then he looks at me and asks again, "Do you want to talk about Jessica?"

I answer bluntly, "I do not."

This bold question leaves our conversation dangling out in the ocean air, deflated. Then he takes his cue, stands up, hugs me a good long while and whispers into my ear, "I'm very pleased we are neighbors and hope this continues." He lifts my chin, looks at my face, "Now you take care darlin', see you tomorrow."

I melt, lean in towards him and put my head on his chest and breath in his manly man scent. Our friendship is aglow with obvious chemistry, and we are both smitten.

CHAPTER SEVEN

School begins again and with that comes excitement, new shoes and new clothes. Jessica is polite and fearless. She is happy and looks forward to her days at Steps. She jumps and walks along next to me. We pass by Sam's window. He steps outside and says, "Have a great day Jessica."

She stops, turns back, holding her Minnie Mouse lunch box and waves goodbye. Life is fun, and I feel younger then I have in years. Life is precious with everything and everyone in my circle.

Hard to grasp how the years fly by. We repeat this scene many times as she learns, grows taller and gains confidence.

CHAPTER EIGHT

Snow and Ash

One Saturday morning, lying around in our pajamas, we hear the lock on the door jiggle. Dana Bea uses her key, pushes the front door open and rushes towards me with urgency in her voice, she orders me to sit down.

She and Coach have been married for one year now, and I thought our early morning conversation might be her announcement of pregnancy. I wait with excitement.

She scans the room, reaches into her satchel, pulls out a coloring book purchased from a local gas station, and hands Jessie a box of new crayons with large print on the side, *Petro Plus*. Jessie eats her cereal and colors in her new book at the same time. I look my daughter square in the eyes, see her fright, toss a shawl over my pajamas, and grab two coffees. We tell Jessie we'll be just outside on the patio.

CHAPTER EIGHT

Her unexpected visit is much more than pregnancy news, something has happened.

"Mom, the realtor who sold your home in Dunsmuir called me this morning. Remember, you gave her my contact information when you moved? She says she has been looking for you. She wants you to know about a house fire in your old neighborhood. Mom, the house that burned to the ground is the run down house around the corner, the one with a vintage car in the driveway."

Dana Bea repeats what the realtor said to her verbatim. "No one was hurt, the occupants managed to jump out of their windows with minimal burns."

The realtor told Dana Bea that the news reported the couple also have a young daughter who is missing. She said the fire inspector made note that no corpse was found in the ash or rubble. The occupants were treated for burns and released from the local hospital. The police located them resting at the Jesus Center. Neither one had any idea what happened to their daughter, who would be eight this year.

My mouth goes dry.

Dana Bea goes on, "The realtor said the neighbors say the child has not been seen or heard from in years. There is an all-out investigation and the parents will be detained tonight."

"Mom, you need to run, go, leave as soon as possible."

I take her by the hand, look into her eyes then look toward the ocean and take a minute to think, while squeezing my daughter's trembling hands. "I disagree honey," Jessica is settled into school, I have her birth certificate and guardianship papers to prove I am her, I am, well, ah, her guardian."

Dana Bea reaches over, grips both my shoulders, shakes me and says, "Mother, we had those made up, they're fake!"

In earshot of Jessie a loud roar comes up from within, "Oh God."

Jessie runs outside, frightened. We assure her everything is fine. I explain that Aunt Dana Bea has some news to tell me. "It's of no concern to you Jessie." She seems relieved, walks back inside and continues on with her coloring project.

"Mom, the realtor says the police are going to talk to you too, because you lived there and moved so abruptly."

Feeling weak in the knees, I stare at my daughter, then put both hands over my eyes and blurt out, "I can't believe this. A damn fire! Those misfits caused a fire and are now homeless. Thank goodness she was not in that filthy house when it was burning, while her parents jump to safety. They can't even smoke without burning down their house!"

Dana Bea scoots her chair close to mine and takes my hands. She squeezes them together, and whispers, "It'll be okay, we'll figure this out."

I question her, "How do the police know I moved quickly?"

"Did you say the realtor knows you are my daughter? I gave her your phone number honey, as my contact person. For all she knows, you are my property manager, secretary, or legal advisor. I never once said you are my daughter. Something is fishy."

CHAPTER EIGHT

She and I sit and stare. I stew in my juices and begin to fume. Dana Bea patiently sits and waits for something; a sign, or an idea, but nothing comes forth.

I am too numb to agree, nod or argue. With a deep breath I ask her if she can take Jessica home for a few hours, or maybe for the night, and take her to school tomorrow. No, school is out, oh right, it's all okay, just leave her be, I can handle coloring, it might be the best medicine for me.

Tears stream down my face, I look up and ask, "Do you know of anyone who can help us, anyone? Let's find someone who might take her in. You are right, we do need to pack her things, and hide her."

Dana Bea waits with me until I decide which direction to turn. I begin to sort, fold clothes, and pack with a vengeance. Dana Bea decides to take Jessie right then, with everything. She takes three bags full of her belongings.

I give Jessie a big hug and whisper, "See you soon sweetie, Aunt Dana Bea will explain everything."

Dana Bea looks back at me and quietly says, "Gee thanks."

In the evening, I crumble, step outside and let out a mournful cry into the night air. Sam dashes outside and scoops me up into his arms.

He asks, "Is it Jessie?"

I tell him the entire farfetched story, from beginning to end. "I am boxed into a corner and they are closing in, and Sam your job is complete, you got us."

Sam holds me tight, we sway back and forth, then he softly and sarcastically says he takes no offense to my comment. "No one got you, no one has found you. You can do this, take the night off, cry your soul out but tomorrow, pull it together and we will make this nightmare go away."

He thinks for a bit and tells me Hansen's wife is a teacher. He says he will ask them if they can help. She is not teaching while they are in California, but can home school Jessie.

Consumed with only thoughts of Jessica, I dismiss Sam's idea and go deaf. I quickly tell him, "I've never been privy to her real name. I have no idea what her first or last name is, or was." And babble on.

He sits and thinks, it is getting late, but he phones his friend Hansen anyway, and tells him we have a problem. We need help and we need you to come over and meet with us tomorrow morning. It is all set into motion. I phone Dana Bea who is hesitant and worries for Jessie to live with strangers.

His friends from Texas are so abstract that no one will ever suspect. I finally feel a tiny smidgen of hope.

Sam walks towards me, takes my hands and holds them to his chest and says with his deep drawl, "This is what's going to happen. The investigators will find you. They will come here to visit. You don't know about the fire. If you tell them someone called your daughter, then you have just made yourself look suspicious and you have also implicated your daughter. If you admit you have a daughter, then she will be next on their list for questioning." Sam explains.

CHAPTER EIGHT

Sam takes charge and continues on, "Say nothing, listen to them, and ask them why they are here. Ask these men to conduct their business so you can get on with your life. Offer nothing."

Sam asks, "Answer this, does Jessica have the same last name as you and Dana Bea?"

I tell him that when we first named her, we did give her our last name, but then after giving it some thought we decided on a different last name to not leave a paper trail. She has a different last name from us. Dana Bea changed her last name on the very day she met the counterfeiter, who made up the birth certificate and guardianship papers. "Jessica's last name is Anderson. Not even close to our last name, Lane. Anderson is less suspicious if a search begins, and to our horror, it has." I state the obvious.

"Did you ever have Jessie finger printed?" Sam asks.

"No, never."

"Then I don't see a paper trail darlin'."

I am so thankful to have Sam in our corner, a former Texas Ranger of all things.

He looks at me and says, "It not over yet."
Sam states, "I suspect these investigators are more concerned with the biological parents' lifestyle than a grieving widow around the corner." Together we think of possible scenarios that might lead to Jessica.

Sam says, "Let your daughter continue to be obscure, continue to work, grocery shop and so on, and you go about your routine too.

Wait it out." Sam suggests. "They won't have the manpower or money to stalk you."

My daughter is in a panic, and so am I, we shake from within.

I trust Sam, whom I hardly know. This is evident when I put Jessica's future in his hands. I have no one else to turn to and we have no alternative.

I make every effort not to alarm Jessica. I make up a story about Nettie having some important business to take care of. Jessica begins to stay with Hansen and Connie. Connie was a fourth grade teacher while living in Texas and she will help Jessie with homework.

We decide to let Jessica stay in Steps. I call Steps and inform them that I will be out of town for a while and that Connie will be taking care of Jessica while I am gone. Connie will pick her up and deliver her to school as they live out of the car pool range. Once the coast is clear she will return home, here, to us, her family, and resume her life on the beach.

Sam comes over one evening and tells me he did his homework, and broke the rules. He gained information on the missing child in Dunsmuir. Some of the information is in today's local paper, regarding the recent fire and missing girl.

"I know her name, the name she had before the wind blew her your way. Do you want to know what it is?"

I take a hard swallow and nod yes, "Yes say it, please." I wait, he stares back at me to make sure I'm ready.

CHAPTER EIGHT

"Holly Clute. Her father goes by Rich, mother Robin. They are legally known as Richard and Robin Clute."

Two weeks later I hear a knock on my front door. Two men in suits introduce themselves and tell me I have a million-dollar view. "Thank you." I politely reply.

I am gracious and invite them in for coffee, and ask, "Now what exactly is this visit about?" Without hesitation they ask me if I know the whereabouts of a little girl named Holly Clute. She is from Dunsmuir, Northern California, where you once lived. She is eight years old. She lived with her parents who lived around the corner from your house." They press on.

I look at them and ask, "You two drove all this way to ask me about a neighbor's child?"

"I wish I could help you find her; I have never heard her name before," I lie. Then ask, "How long has she been missing?"

"Holly went missing as a toddler."

I play it sweet, and as dumb a fox. I also try to not vomit into the potted plant next to the sofa.

Sam is next door listening through the wall with a glass up to his ear. He listens as they continue to ask more questions, and he hears my replies with nondescript answers. They go over the dates of my move from the north state to my present location.

In a calm voice I answer, "Yes, that is correct, I did move here at that time."

SNOW AND ASH

They want to know why I chose this location, so far away. My response is truthful, "I enjoy the ocean and the central location."

"Why did you move so abruptly?" They ask.

I tell them about my husband's passing. How I searched for peace and in doing so, decided to change towns. Over the years I searched many states and towns to relocate, to begin a new life as a widow. This amazing property came up and I grabbed it as fast as possible." They ask me his name. "Jim Lane." I say in a soft voice. I am positive they will check death records in Siskiyou county. Which is fine.

We continue to talk in circles and I can never thank Sam enough for practicing this interview with me, several times.

We shake hands, they look around the place and leave. I plop down on the couch and almost faint. I talk to my heart and tell it to settle down, and order myself to breath deep.

One point bothers me; how did they know I moved quickly? I suspect the realtor.

Suddenly I feel a tickle on the back of my ankle, I leap straight up with fright, bend down to look. Staring back at me is the trunk of the pink elephant sticking out from under the sofa.

Instead of agonizing at the thought of being caught, my only concern is for Jessie, who is staying with friends and she forgot to take her pink elephant.

The next day I place the fuzzy elephant in a shoe box and hand it to Sam, to deliver to Jessie. Just in case they are taking photos outside,

CHAPTER EIGHT

Sam decides to transfer it into a paper sack with celery sticks poking out of the top.

The day we allowed Sam to step into our lives has been a test of trust for me and Dana Bea. To some degree, she and I expect him to handcuff us and lead us away to an unmarked car, then wait for him to deliver Jessica back to her low-life raging parents, tip his hat and say goodbye. Meanwhile she and I are funneled out the side doors of the courthouse with chains on our wrists and ankles, to be finger printed. But so far he has proven to be an honest Texan with a sexy crooked smile.

We know what we are doing is wrong on many levels, against the law, and none of our business. We were not longing for adventure. Dana Bea and I closed our eyes and dove in head first, and in doing so we both did a full swan dive into a life of crime. I don't regret one single day. Jessica is worth saving and protecting, and I will go to the ends of the earth to keep her parents from getting her back.

Paranoia planted its seed and is now in full bloom. I watch tourists walking along the beach and quiver at the sight of them being possible undercover agents. My binoculars are getting worn out from my intense daily scrutiny. I keep a vigil for secret spies, men and women; who comb the beach and pretend to hunt for shells.

It is a minute by minute struggle to accept this lifestyle. You can't fool your brain.

Sam sends Hansen on a mission; to drive up to the North State and snoop around. Hansen does this for Sam. He leaves for a week. He said he looked around and asked neighbors about the toddler who went missing in the early '80s. He also went downtown and asked around at coffee shops and the local bar, The Dunsmuir Brewery. No one seems to have any details or ideas. He thinks the two guys who drove down to question me were grasping. Hoping for a long shot. I feel safer than before, but always on high alert and always filled with worry.

CHAPTER NINE

Broken Glass

ONE DAY MIDWEEK THERE IS A KNOCK AT THE DOOR. There stands a man in shorts wearing a Hawaiian shirt. He asks if he can use my phone, "It's an emergency, my car has a dead battery." I don't believe him for one second. He is a spy and is trying to get to my phone to plant a bug, and right front of me.

He gives me the creeps and I tell him, "No, sorry," and close the door.

He sticks his foot inside to block the door from closing. I struggle to reach for something to make noise, to alert someone. He pushes his way in, grabs my shoulders and tosses me to the sofa. I begin to fight and scream but he quickly puts his hand across my mouth. I do the only thing I am able to do. I reach with my left arm to grab the nearest weapon, a heavy glass paper weight that sits on the window sill to catch the light. My fingers curl around the paperweight as he rips my dress and pushes his body over mine. My dress is pulled up around my waist and he punches me several times in the face. I feel warm blood running down my face and into my ears. I reach back and hit the window with the thick glass paperweight, which makes

CHAPTER NINE

the front large window shatter. The attacker rips and pulls at my dress and rips off my underpants. I try to scream and move my head from side to side to get his hand off my mouth. I struggle to kick, but he has his legs between mine. I am immobile.

Suddenly the rapist is pulled off of me as if an alien from the sky has him by the buttocks. He swooshes up and away towards the ceiling. I see the edge of an arm, a large tan arm. It's Sam. My neighbor punches him in the face, picks him up by the throat. The intruder kicks Sam between the legs. This causes Sam to double over and moan. I crawl to the phone and dial the police. Sam sticks out his leg and trips the guy as he tries to flee. Sam flips him over, then sits on top of him, on his backside with his knee on his spine and pounds his head into the floor.

I hear sirens, and we both huff and puff and wait for help. Sam sits on top of the attacker, holding both of his arms and waits. I put a cloth to my bleeding nose and face. This police rescue is about unlawful entry and a physical attack. We hear fast steps running up the stairs in front of our homes, and slowly we hear broken glass crackle as footsteps cross over a once bay window. A warning is called out, and slowly the front door bursts open.

Sam yells, "He's under control."

With guns drawn they cautiously step inside. I tell them, "The man on the floor is the attacker." They bend down, put handcuffs on the intruder while Sam straddles him and regrettably relinquishes his grip.

They haul him away; he stumbles off the steps with his limp head hanging down. Sam introduces himself to the officers as my neighbor. They ask me if I need to go to the hospital but I decline.

We do agree go to the police station and give our statements. In the meantime, the landlord tapes plywood across the front window and arranges for a new duel pane replacement, a crew is on the way to clean up all the glass. My treasured glass paperweight is lost forever; it must have rolled down the rocks.

Sam and I look at each other and pretend we are just neighbors, not involved, which actually we are not, and continue to answer questions. The black and blue marks begin to reveal his grip on my forearms and my knee cap has a nice long cut, probably from the window. My face is swollen and turns black and blue. They snap photos. I tell them I'll put a cold pack on it when I get home and phone my physician.

We go to his place, and curl up into a ball on the couch while he boils water for hot tea. I begin to shake, unable to hold my tea. He drops to his knees and wraps his big arms around my shivering body, and out of nowhere I begin to sob. The toll of these past months, and years of illegal flight and an unprovoked attack came bubbling out of my eyes and mouth. The tension releases a buildup of long wet drips flowing down my cheeks, and saliva seeps out of the corners of my mouth and onto his chest. Sam gently cleans the blood off my face and places an ice pack on my forehead.

The crying lasts far longer than it should. He pets my back while I shake and whimper. He coos and comforts me as if I am the baby and he the father. I wipe my nose on his shirt and notice his knuckles. They are scrapped up and covered with dried blood. He doesn't say a word.

The sun sets and I don't want to go home.

This is the first night I spend with Sam. He holds me in his arms all night, and I sleep like a baby, feeling completely safe and at peace. Unable to relinquish my torn dress, I curl up and sleep in it all night. His soft rhythmic snore lulls me deeper into a rich sleep. He doesn't touch me, no wandering hands, he simply offers the protection and closeness that I have longed for since Jim's passing.

CHAPTER NINE

The next morning over coffee Sam softly tells me the attack could have been very brutal and possibly fatal. He cautions me to be very careful.

"When there is a knock at your door, look out your window, do not unlock and open your door. Ask for credentials."

"You are one lucky lady. He is apprehended, in jail, and he will never again think this is a secluded place and easy pickings for an attack. You must tell Dana Bea about this attack so she will also be prepared, God forbid something like this might come her way. You never know when and where this could happen."

I finally get the nerve to phone her, but not for a few days. On Friday, because my daughter won't have to work the next day when I tell her this horrendous story. I know my girl and she will not be able to sleep. As I predict, she is mortified. The news of the attacker in a jail cell, and the fact that I am not injured eases her concerns. Sam also ads his two cents and assures Dana Bea and Coach that all is well on the bluff. That night, after dinner there is a knock at the door, I peek between the curtains and there stands Dana Bea with her duffle bag. She has arrived for a sleep over.

Jessica was with Connie and Hansen. They bring her back home to visit and we pretend not to be traumatized or jumpy. The girls put ice on my face and I gently tell them a nicer gentler version of the assault, but Dana Bea knows the difference.

We three cuddle up together. Well, the cuddling began that way. Dana Bea gets claustrophobic and breaks away from our clinging arms. She jumps out of bed and crawls into Jessie's bed, and nestles in her little alcove for the rest of the night.

A week later the police knock on my door. I immediately think they are going to arrest me for being a kidnapper. They are here to deliver information on the attacker. They tell me his name, and show me his long rap sheet for minor arrests, brutal attacks and one rape. I swallow hard and know how close I came to being his next victim.

Sam walks in and introduces himself as a former Texas Ranger. Everyone shakes hands and there is an air of awe in the room. They nod and say they are pleased to meet him. Sam again reaches out with his big tan hand and shakes each officer's hand saying, "Likewise."

The police tell me there will be a court hearing coming up, and they will alert me of the date. I stand there like a wet noodle and finally ask them if the attacker is in jail now or out on bail. They tell me he is being held in jail until his court date. He is a flight risk with priors, and no bail has been set.

The court date arrives and I identify the attacker. Sam stands next to me as if he is the unassuming helpful neighbor We leave in separate cars. Sam arrives a little after me at my place with two fresh coffees and a box full of donuts.

Because of the attack, my world still spins and I feel vulnerable and exposed. We decide to let Jessica stay with Hansen and Connie, for a few more days, then she will return. No one has contacted us from the North State and no one seems to be lurking around on the beaches. We had decided to wait it out a while but I can't stand it any longer and feel it's not healthy for Jessie to live with so many secrets. She must pick up on something, she's not a robot.

Sam agrees and gives me an extra tight hug. We are united in our fight to continue on as the nice neighboring couple on the top of the rocky bluff.

CHAPTER NINE

Thanksgiving is delicious and quick. We have our meal at a famous chef's house known as Dana Bea's, along with Coach, the assistant cook. Hansen and Connie arrive too. Jessica is happy to see them, and the rest of the day is filled with nibbling, playing board games and the sounds of a football game in the background We celebrate together, as one big family. Nice, casual and comfortable. Now we wait for her birthday, then Christmas. I shop and knit in a frenzy while Sam runs on the beach, which is a sight to behold. I fuss around the tiny house and wish I knew something about the case; not the one from the intruder in my home, but the one concerning Jessica. My constant fear of being discovered is madness that is effecting all our lives. Something needs to change.

CHAPTER TEN

Undercover

DANA BEA AND COACH TAKE A MINI VACATION to enjoy snow skiing at Mt. Shasta. During this time, they'll ski, dine in Dunsmuir and snoop around my old neighborhood. One stormy day they nix the snow skiing and decide to check out Shady Lane. Coach cruises in front of my once cozy 1950s style home, then he drives around the corner and Dana Bea snaps photos of the burnt out house. She reports back to me that the neighbors act the same; staying indoors and uncommitted to drama or any signs of life. My previous home also indicates no signs of life. Being the reporter she is, Dana Bea has Coach circle back so she can jump out of the car and snap a photo of my once coiffured yard. This is good thinking because she now has a photo of the porch and the Dogwood that stands at the end of the porch, the exact spot where I rescued my sweet Jessie. She turns around and snaps a photo of the clump of pines, then runs down the street and takes another photo to show the proximity between the Dogwood and pines.

CHAPTER TEN

When they round the corner she takes note of black soot that was once a house. The ash is now covered with snow and appears to be a piece of art, with remnants of a once brick fireplace. Dana Bea snaps many photos and she also takes a picture of the blackened shell of a car. Today, Rich's beloved vintage investment is an eye sore.

Dana Bea and Coach stop in to chat with the realtor. Pretending to be shopping for real estate, Dana Bea casually asks about a news story they had read. She asks how the investigation is going and mentions the rubble on Shady Lane. Dana Bea is informed the police are focusing on the parents and strongly suspect they are responsible for their daughter's demise. They think the child died from neglect or was killed and buried someplace in the forest. They suspect she died accidently while in her parents' care. But without a body, it's all speculation. This realtor, has her finger on the pulse of this small town. She tells Dana Bea that the parents are pretending they have no idea what happened to their daughter. "Their stance of ignorance is causing them a lot of flack with the police but they are not investigating in further." Changing direction to a more sellable subject the realtor asks, "How's the snow?"

Dana Bea gets ready to answer when clever Coach jumps in, "Truly awesome. You ski?" He asks.

"When I was younger, but not anymore," she replies. The next fifteen minutes of small talk continues to mislead the realtor to the false hope of potential buyers. They chat about the snow pack, the ski lodge, great runs and the length of time they have been ski enthusiasts.

There is no mention of the nice widow who moved so abruptly nor any connection of her to Dana Bea and Coach.

UNDERCOVER

Dana Bea hands me a stack of photos, to show Jessica one day. I observe, "Snow and ash, thank you honey, this set of photos are perfect for her file."

Lea, continues to come over to play with Jessica, and their friendship blooms. The blessing is, they look alike, same color hair, same long golden waves and body types. I hope the watchful eyes who sit in the shadows are a bit confused and mixed up with these twins. There I go again, being paranoid.

Seems a long time until Spring. We continue to dodge imagined stalkers and keep Jessie secure. We feel the air getting warmer, and the days on the calendar are marked with an X, to show Jessie the time frame for summer play.

While Jessie is at school Sam heads a meeting between us. The players include; his ex-partner Hansen and his wife Connie, Dana Bea with her clear thinking criminal mind, me with my paranoia, and lots of coffee.

The Rangers talk about the facts, the surveillance, the ongoing investigation, Jessica and the coming year. Hansen volunteers to take another run up north to prowl around, look at the local newspaper's archive vault and talk to the police. I offer to pay for his lodging, food and gas. We do need to know how the investigation is really going. Hansen's idea to snoop around can only be positive, he knows what he is doing. We all knew not to blindly trust the opinion of a talkative onlooker such as the realtor. We send Hanson on his way.

Hansen is gone for a week and returns with good news. Just like the realtor had said, the investigation is closed.

CHAPTER TEN

Another meeting is scheduled, I am to pick up Jessie at Lea's and drive her to Connie and Hansen's home. When I return home from delivering Jessie to Connie, Sam sits me down on the couch, Dana Bea curls up at the other end. Hansen sits close by. They gather around me and gently let me know that I am paranoid, and overly cautious. My behavior effects many, and its time to relax and join the living. You must realize you are not being followed, and you are not on America's most wanted list.

I feel trapped and betrayed. I sit very still, look and listen. I never imagined an intervention. I have done nothing wrong. I am trying to keep us safe. My chest heaves up, and I slowly let out stress and anger. I sit and wait for a confidence bubble to pop out of my brain and into my mouth, and it does. "I will take this chance, I will try to not look over my shoulder any longer, and I won't mistrust the human race. I will do this for Jessica's sake." I make this promise while I think to myself, "It is a fatal mistake to wear blinders."

Lea's parents think our friends, where Jessie often stays are her aunt and uncle. She actually loves to visit their home. Connie has a nurturing spirit, who loves to teach positive communication and understanding skills. This makes Dana Bea and I feel lower than dirt as we sprinkle this child with lies. Telling lies has become so easy, I begin to believe them myself.

Jessie is a smart and resilient girl. Lea and she get along like sisters and this is comforting for all of us. Jessie is getting curious about her life, our relationship and begins to question who I am to her. I know the time is growing near, and one day she will demand the truth, and the truth she will hear. She will soon witness her file.

UNDERCOVER

School zooms by and so do the years. Jessica is growing taller and she has a very pleasant way about her, but she is no one's fool.

In August Dana Bea and I take Jessica shopping and buy new school clothes, socks, shoes and a new lunch box with a unicorn running under a rainbow. School begins, and shortly after she is promoted to a combo class of fifth and sixth graders. Jessica is now ahead of her class in most subjects. I struggle to relax, but say nothing. Sam senses my ongoing concern.

Our family and extended family, Connie and Hansen, decide to go for an adventure, see some sights. We decide to take advantage of our area and its history. We drive south and tour the San Luis Obispo Mission. It is a mission founded in 1772 by father Juniper Serra. It is the fifth mission in a chain of twenty-one missions dotting along the California coastline and valleys.

This tour is something I have wanted to do for years. Connie and Hansen make the plans. Most fourth graders in California schools have an assignment to choose a mission then make a replica using cardboard, straw, paper, paint and any other materials that will help their construction resemble their mission. Some missions have a well and a little bucket, a rope to pull up the well water, some kids cut paper squares to make a red tile roof and some have fences made of tooth picks. It is a great accomplishment to make these designs.

Today, the mission we visit has a lovely stream that moves slowly along not far from the mission, which is also a museum. The mission is so small. The door ways, and arches are so tiny even I have to bend over to walk inside. The window looking out is also small. It is such a great feeling to relive this time of life and imagine living there.

CHAPTER TEN

We sit under trees by the creek and have lunch after our tour. We choose to sit outside in the courtyard, absorb the information, enjoy the mountain range and imagine this area in 1772. We drink lemon tea from a thermos and munch on crackers, cheese, and a bag of fresh cut vegetables.

I have been watching Jessie throughout the day; her features and her expressions. I notice what a wonderful lady unfolds before my eyes. She is thankful, polite and enthusiastic. I feel a warm rush come over me and try to hide my tears.

I take a bite from a cracker with cheese on the top. Then, from out of the blue I hear a young voice, "Oh Nettie." Jessica's arms wrap around my neck. I pat her arms that loop across my chest This sweet moment engulfs me, and we sweetly continue on with our luncheon, despite any dysfunctional dynamics.

Back again, and in the car, as the sun begins to set. Dana Bea drives through a fast food place and says she can't live on crackers and cheese. Dana Bea pulls over under the shade of a huge oak tree and we gobble down some non-nutritional fast foods.

Our friends leave in their own car, we wave and go our separate ways. Jessie opens a gift we hid under the backseat. A thick, ultra-soft blanket of powder blue. I think as we ride in Dana Bea's messy car with cheese and shredded lettuce everywhere, "Today has been a special fun day." I feel great, *except for those two guys in a car that pulled out just after we left with our food.* I take a deep breath and let it slide so as not to ruin the day. I know my imagination has formed a habit of expansion and wide scale drama. My vibe causes Dana Bea to peek out the back window, then tell me, "They are gone."

She repeats, "No men. Mom, it's not against the law for two males to sit in a car together."

"I would hate to be exposed as a synthetic family and will fight to the end to keep us together." I whisper to Dana Bea.

"Mother, chill out, seriously, you are going to make yourself sick," Dana Bea demands.

Connie who often keeps Jessie for sleep overs cares for her deeply. She also keeps an eye out, and knows how to get in touch with me when need be. This is one less thing I have to worry about. Thank Heaven I am not the only one who can see the potential danger of kidnapping a child. I think to myself and mumble. Connie must have learned to keep a keen eye out, and be aware of her surroundings from her husband. I pretend to be confident and learn from her.

Dana Bea pulls into her garage; Jessica runs into the family room to watch cartoons. We see nothing out of order, no phone calls, no men lurking in the shadows. Maybe it's just me, seeing what is not there. I walk into the kitchen and sigh; Jessie falls asleep on the sofa.

With a pinch of luck and a glint of conviction I try to let go of my feelings of danger around every corner. Dana Bea reminds me that we don't need luck, and today was not a chance of danger. Today was a fabulous outing.

She puts everything from her car into a garbage bag; left over snacks, papers, Mission information, wrapping paper and directions. She secures it with a twisty. Then she brings it into her house and decides to not dispose of it in her garbage can, it's too public. She says she will take the bag to work. I watch and wonder with sadness, what I have done to my daughter, she lives like a criminal, and a clever one

CHAPTER TEN

at that. We say our goodbyes, hug and I drive back to my home, alone. Jessie is thrilled to spend the night with her Aunt. I drive back to the beach and think back to my daughter and her bag of garbage; She is as paranoid as I am, but refuses to admit it.

It's late, I drive up to my parking lot, grab my suede purse and dart towards the stairs. In a running jog I sprint to the top; Sam steps out. He is worried sick and says he has been pacing and waiting for a long time.

This is so sweet and endearing for such a big rough man; To act timid. We sit down on the patio chairs, I wrap a huge cotton shawl around my shoulders while he brings us hot mint tea. I tell him about our day, and in midsentence he slowly leans forward, and deliberate. He takes his large weathered tan finger and moves a curl off my forehead and tucks it in behind my ear. His hand touches another curl on my neck. I have no idea what I am saying and immediately become tongue tied. He leans in, close to my face and kisses my lips. A soft tender moment makes way for a passionate kiss that seems to last a while, the waves hit the shore and the night air begins to move my curls back into my face. He reaches for my lap, picks up my hand and leads me to his duplex. We step into his place, out of the ocean's night air. I take my shawl and pull it in real close around my shoulders, then turn and look at Sam, we lock eyes and the shawl drops to the floor. Sam takes two steps toward me, engulfs me in his arms and I melt.

The next morning, I wake up with a wide silly grin across my face and bury my face into his pillow, take in his scent and search for my confidence and maturity; *and my dress.* He slips out from between the sheets, takes five steps to his kitchen. I listen to him clang the pans, and take in the smell of coffee and bacon. I sneak a peek at him and pleasantly witness this huge burly man standing in his boxers cooking us breakfast. Oh to hell with it, I love this scene. I fluff up both pillows to get a better view.

He saunters over with two muffins and a couple pieces of bacon then returns with our coffee. We get crunchy bacon crumbs all over the sheets, slowly sip our coffee and quietly talk.

It doesn't take long to eat this meal, and after we finish I collapse and fall onto his lap and roll around like a rolly polly with no concern of how I look. I am giggling and more silly than I have ever been before.

He laughingly says, "Now settle down little filly, you might fall off the bed."

We laugh together like two silly kids; me with my messy upside down hair, and Sam with that crooked smile. I am not concerned with ever loosing Sam. I know he will always be here for me and so far he is living up to and beyond my expectations.

We have a month before school begins again. I normally would be cooking and cleaning but this new level our friendship has taken on now has a life of its own, and this knocks me off balance. I struggle to focus while my head swirls in the clouds.

Once again Dana Bea and Coach take Jessie out on a fishing boat. I sure hope she doesn't get sea sickness like she did the first time out. With her away for the day, Sam and I decide to clean up the place. We begin to wash windows, clean the hardwood floors. He puts a light coat of paint in the alcove where Jessica has her twin bed. Now her alcove is powder blue.

CHAPTER TEN

I make a run to the grocery store to stock our kitchen and wait for our sunbaked girl to come home. The door flings open, their skin is rosy pink, and all three talk at once. I heat up some food to enjoy as we sit around the place and listen to sea stories. They watched large fish following along with their boat, were surrounded by a family of dolphins, and then the inevitable story about the big one that got away.

Jessie loves her new freshly painted alcove. She showers, has a hot meal, jumps in her bed and curls up with her new ultra-soft blanket and reads. Dana Bea and Coach leave for home.

Sam and I have no idea what to do about *us*. Most evenings are spent on my deck or his. We sit across from each other, rub our toes together and sip wine. This is a peculiar relationship, and we wish for an easier path. I suggest we enjoy what we have, enjoy what we can, and relish this fabulous adventure. Which is much better than a movie.

Our situation beckons us to another evening of watching the sun slowly retreat into darkness, while the waves continue to roll up to the shore, then pull back into the night. Sam still calls me darlin', but now he adds the endearing term, my darlin' companion. I love our connection.

Tomorrow is the first day of school. Later in the month is open house, followed by parent teacher meetings, and back to school night. Here we go Jessie girl.

CHAPTER ELEVEN

Blending Our Love

THREE YEARS PASS BY SO QUICKLY is seems we have been asleep. Three more birthdays, and another three New Year's Eves. I can't help but notice Jessica sprouting up. I wonder where she gets her height. Fun times with a teenager. She is curvy and has an athletic body. Her hair has grown long and her group of friends bubble over. She is getting older and more mature and so are we. She and Lea practice dance moves and make-up application every time they are together, which is every day.

Dana and Coach have been married for over four years, and have a son, Charlie Rex. This is a very special time for them, but more for me. She invited me into the delivery room to witness the birth of my grandson.

Charlie is growing fast and being attentive parents, they take him cross country skiing in Oregon so they can visit Coach's family and ski. Coach has Charlie in many sports programs, while Mama Dana Bea teaches him table manners.

CHAPTER ELEVEN

Coach has managed to get Jessica on a traveling volleyball team. He coaches her and she is a monster on the court. She is competitive and has the muscles to slam down hard on the other team, she also does great set ups to teammates. It is exhilarating to sit in the bleachers and watch her games. She is strong and determined. Sam yells louder than everyone else.

Sam slipped on the wet steps one morning and twisted his ankle. He uses a cane now and I hold onto the rail these days. I have stopped sprinting and showing off as I used to, running up or down the steps, passing by Sam's window in a blur.

Jessie says she needs to talk to Sam, alone and personal. I understand teens and let her have her space. Later Sam asks where is this coming from and I have to say, "I guess she has always wanted to ask you something, but was too shy."

Sam said that Jessie got up the nerve, after beating around the bush and hem hawing around. She shyly asked him if it would be okay if she calls him Grandpa. He is so proud of this, and says it is an honor and he is proud to answer to that name. They shook hands on this deal.

The sound of her sweet young voice yelling out, "Hi Grandpa," as she runs down the steps, on her way to school is heartwarming. The energy and intense mood swings of youth fill our small home with love, song and stories.

Sam has convinced me that I am not being followed. I try to stop worrying as I promised but I still keep an eye out for anyone or anything that might seem out of place. Jessie stays close to home or I drive her to a friend's house. She never walks alone.

This Sunday, while washing and drying dishes with Jessie, she stops, turns, looks at me and asks, "Where did I come from?" I almost drop my plate. "Why am I in a private school?"

Unprepared, I pull the stored mother tapes out of my head and answer, "One day you will understand. One day I will tell you everything and explain this information in great detail. Let's just get you raised, okay Jessie?"

She is disappointed, she sits down, hangs her head and stares at her lap, and quietly asks, "Can you tell me anything, just one thing?"

I stop, set down my kitchen towel, hold her in place and touch her shoulders. In soft but firm voice I answer her question, "I saved you Jessie."

She hugs me with her soapy hands and whispers, "I thought so."

In her mature mind, Jessie stops to notify me that it is time to stop sprinkling pink and blue toppings on the cookies.

Then we move on and have a grandpa talk. She cuddles in close and I begin. "Grandpa Sam loves you, and he takes care of you in more ways than you know. Sometimes you can be a grandpa just by being loyal and true. He is your grandpa and will be forever." She likes these talks, so I go on to say "He will be honest with every question you will ever ask him. You be careful and be prepared for what you wish for or ask. Jessica, he also happens to be a special person in my life too. He protects me, and we talk about everything under the sun. We laugh together, run on the beach, or at least we used to run together, now we walk.

CHAPTER ELEVEN

Jessie smiles and asks, "Do you kiss?"

I swallow hard, "Now missy, let's not be nosey." We both giggle.

"Sometimes we do kiss, and I want you to know that grandpa Sam is my boyfriend because he is a boy and because he is a friend."

"Oh Nettie, I have heard that line before, and it is so silly." She giggles, and takes a huge bite out of her cookie, she then makes one with a huge pink heart on top, runs next door—a gift to Grandpa Sam.

I'm thinking, "Oh boy! Jessie has developed radar and night goggles. Ol' Sam and I better watch our night moves."

The following year Jessie is dressing for school. I can't help but notice she is becoming a young woman. Her eyes are beautiful, deep blue. Her hair has darkened and her body is beginning to get curvy. This metamorphoses into a young lady will open a whole new set of worries. Boys will begin to come around, and thank heaven she is not old enough to date, not by a long shot. She has a perky personality, and Grandpa Sam keeps a close eye on her activities. We question her more when she asks to go out with friends.

Dana Bea, the eternal bride is busy raising her son Charlie, who looks just like his mom, who in turn, looks like her dad Jim. He is so cute and verbal, he is a little chatter box and all boy.

Sam decides that we should all go as a family, see some sights and stop somewhere to eat. Off we go in two cars. We drive south past San Luis Obispo, then Los Osos and continue on. We visit the Ostrich farm in

Solvang. There, they let us feed the ostriches and this is great fun. They show us the ostrich eggs, which appear to be the size of a Volkswagen.

We continue on, Sam pulls into The Museum of Cowboys. Dana and I walk together while Coach chases after Charlie. Sam still walks with a cane and Jessie, is always close by his side. We pay and walk into a building that looks like a barn. We study black and white photos of famous well known Cowboys. Also a photo display of black cowboys who are relatively unknown. This non-descript barn-like museum is fascinating as we venture along, we turn left, and continue to walk down the hallway to look at stuffed horses, and stuffed rattlesnakes. Very creepy. Then we see behind the glass vintage saddles, cowboy gear, boots, spurs and abused cooking pots from cattle drives. There is a display of an old wooden beaten up card table with worn faded red flannel material on top. Well used vintage playing cards lay on the table as if the cowboys just stepped away.

We enjoy colorful conversations after our tour, and share ideas of the times long past. Outside is a café with tables overlooking the valley. Sam orders food and drinks for us.

Dinner is delicious, and the place is crowded. There is lots of chatter, laughter, and music. The songs are country western and this sets the stage to be rowdy.

We eat Bar B Q ribs, potatoes and onion rings. Charlie has sauce all over his face, and each of us have the same reddish brown smiles on our lips and faces.

Sam stands up, stretches out his arms then drops to his knees. We gasp, Charlie is startled and watches, Jessie lets out a soft scream and reaches for his cane. I sit in fear, unable to respond.

CHAPTER ELEVEN

Sam adjusts himself and says, "No worries." He reaches into his pocket and pulls out a ring box. You could hear a pin drop it was so quiet. The café owners turn off the music. Everyone in the place watches this white haired handsome man when he says, "My sweetheart, would you do me the honor of marrying me?"

I wipe my mouth clean, still unable to speak. Dana Bea sits stunned, she and I seem to be frozen, peering down at Sam.

Coach shouts, "Well answer him. Don't keep that boy on his knees."

I put my hand on his weathered aged tan hands and tell him, "I thought you'd never ask. Oh yes, yes, I will surely marry you Samuel."

We hear lots of noise, cat calls, whistling from the other tables of families, followed by loud applause. Dana Bea smiles and looks at me straight into my face, we read each other's eyes. I nod and smile back. She nods back. Jessie jumps up and quickly helps her grandpa back onto his feet. Everyone claps for him when he stands. Sam sits down and puts his arm around me. I am overjoyed, but also satisfied to just be neighbors. Our relationship has grown to such a comfortable place; but this, well this is simply the icing on the cake.

Fun times—we instantly begin to make wedding to plans. Jessie is all about helping and planning, and Dana Bea wants all the details, and offers to help anyway she can.

We decide to get married in Texas at one of Sam's friends' cattle ranch. He tells us that Ray welcomes us with open arms. We will fly out together, with all the kids.

BLENDING OUR LOVE

Sam tells Ray to make sure the bunk houses are clean and spotless when we arrive. We decide to get married in June, school will be out. June 2nd is the date.

Time seems to zip by at rapid speed. Dana Bea and I go shopping while Jessie is in school. We browse in and out of boutiques, but the dresses are too disco, I just can't do that, even though it's the rage. Then we see a store with a grand opening sign, called Bust a Move.

I confide to my daughter what I have in mind. She smiles with a sarcastic smirk and questions my choices with, "You're kidding right?"

"No, not even a little bit." I whisper.

I tell the salesperson I am a senior citizen getting married. She looks at my daughter and winks. I think to myself, "Do they think I am so old I can't see?" I am on a mission, so I let it slide. I tell Dana Bea what color I want and the material. Dana Bea walks next to me and pats me on the back, like you do when someone is ill, or senile. Then I spot it, hanging on the rack, and in my size too, size 10.

I tell the girl helping us that I'll need a girdle, Dana Bea interrupts and tells me that no one says girdle anymore.

She looks at the sales girl and corrects me, "She means a Spandex."

I chime in, "Yes, I need a full body Spandex."

I step into the dressing room, and it takes a while as I squirm and contort to get my butt into the *girdle* then the dress. Once in it, it fits like a glove. A tight glove. "Sam is going to enjoy trying to get me out of this dress."

CHAPTER ELEVEN

Dana Bea gasps, "Mother please!"

I love it and hand the young woman my credit card. Turn back to my daughter and say, "Now we need to find shoes and have them dyed to match."

Dana Bea warns me not to get too, *"matchy-matchy."*

"What does that mean? I ask.

"It's not what you do." She explains.

"No more matching shoes to a dress?" I ask.

"No, not anymore Mom."

"Okay then, let's find non matching shoes."

I giggle to myself about my outfit and feel as if I am twenty again. We hug and together walk out of Bust a Move, holding my packages.

Leaving out a description of my dress I tell Sam all about our day while Jessica surprises us with dinner. I guess she has been watching while I wasn't paying attention. She is busy chopping vegetables while I talk to Sam. We smell something cooking on the stove, take in the aroma, and try to guess our surprise meal.

He tells me within earshot of Jessica, he will pick out his own clothes. Then adds that he will out dress me by a long shot. Jessie continues to chop foods, stir and giggle.

BLENDING OUR LOVE

Dana Bea then phones to tell me it is all going so fast she can't wrap her head around our big day.

I tell her, "Honey, when you're our age, time is of the essence." She lets out a sigh. This is so much fun. The date is coming up, with just two months to go. We have plane tickets lined up for everyone. We'll fly into Dallas, rent a van then drive to the ranch. Sam explains it's in the middle of nowhere. *This is comforting.*

Everyone gets their finest cowgirl and cowboy outfits together. I enroll Jessie in Horse Camp for the next four weekends, just in case Sam wants to take her out on the plains. Dana Bea signs herself up too. Every Saturday they go to this dude ranch and take riding lessons, while I keep Charlie.

Charlie tells his dad he feels left out. Grandpa Sam assures him he can go for a horsey ride with him, and ride *lots* faster than those ol' girls.

Dana Bea jumps in front of Sam. "Seriously Sam, don't ride fast with my son." He smiles his ornery crooked smile and says, "No worries momma."

Sam's in charge of music and chats with Ray and Peg over the phone about food and shelter for our crew of wedding goers. "No worries." They tell us.

Again I talk to them about food and riding.
"No big deal." And they hang up.

Our gang of Californians decide to stay ten days. I phone back to ask if ten days it too long to stay. "Okay, no big deal." They Click off.

CHAPTER ELEVEN

This place is not a dude ranch. It's the real deal, a working cattle ranch. They are too busy to talk.

Jessie asks if she can bring a friend along, her best friend, Lea. We talk to her parents, and they agree to let her come along with us. They give us a medical release form just in case Lea takes a spill off a horse or something more or less ranch worthy, and they pay her airfare. The girls will *bunk* together, and this all seems to be falling into place.

The week before we leave Lea and Jessie finish up with school. The girls and I go shopping and buy two appropriate sun dresses. They also buy Levis, t-shirts, heavy socks and shorts, just in case there is a change in the weather. They pack lotion that smells like vanilla, and new shampoo called, Royal B shampoo. I pack muscle rub lotions, aspirin, and my camera.

Lea and Jessie go with me to the western store to buy cowboy boots. Jessie and Lea buy new cowboy boots and wear them every day to break them in. Dana Bea buys boots too. Coach says he's going to buy his boots in Texas, Sam chimes in with a loud, "Hell yeah Coach!"

Right on schedule we arrive at the airport, wait, then board the non-stop plane; San Francisco to Dallas. Sam is as calm as he can be, he actually appears smug. I am busy making sure everyone has a packet of snacks, a bottle of water and a small pillow for the flight, and off we go. As we board the plane I sense I'm the only one with concern, a case of nerves. We get situated into our seats. Charlie sits next to me, his parents smile. I look across the aisle to them and mouth, "Thanks." They laugh.

Sam orders a drink, and so does Coach, Dana Bea has ice water. I sit there picking at my fingernails, then reach out with my short arm, stop the stewardess and order a vodka tonic.

We land, wait for luggage, then step out of the Dallas airport. Sam rents a large van and gets into the driver's seat. He is as calm as he can be.

All we see is flat land as far as we look in all directions; it's just like the ocean only beige. "They must have the largest ranch in the United States," I joke. No one laughs.

We finally pull off the main road, then drive down a long dirt road towards a farm house far in the distance. We jump out and stand in awe. It is beautiful, raw, unpretentious and peaceful.

Ray and Peg show us the bunk houses. When the doors open we smell fresh paint. We see new bed spreads with western designs, and new fluffy towels.

Our room is upstairs in the farm house. I am in love with this place, it is amazing. I go on about the big barn, all of the cows, horses and chickens.

Sam shows me where we will stand. He points, "Right over there." "You walk out of the barn over there, and I'll be waitin' by the big oak." He politely asks me if that sounds okay, and I agree.

He asks if I have any special music in mind, but before I reply, he goes on to say he has friends who play in a band and they will be here for the preparation and part of the reception. I am shocked at

CHAPTER ELEVEN

his organization. He goes on to tell me that the help will put out long tables for a Tex-Mex spread.

Sam remembers another piece of information and adds, "During dinner we'll dine to a blue grass band called, Ravens Crow."

The next day Sam and I concoct an idea to put Jessica, Lea and Dana Bea to work on an art project, while Charlie and Coach feed the chickens.

Before we begin to be crafty, we drive into town. At the four way stop, we find a mercantile store and browse awhile. We women take off to find a second-hand store and buy up a bunch of worn out boots. I find a pair in great shape, the same color as my dress and plunk them on top of the counter as fast as lightening. We walk to the local hardware store and purchase cans of spray paint, brushes and tape. We walk around the corner to the only florist shop in town and buy bundles of different types of country flowers.

Inside the barn, we each grab a boot. We dust, and clean, and scrape the heels. We polish them with damp rags and clean the undersides. On top of an old table we begin to spray paint. We paint red boots, blue boots and yellow boots. While the paint is still wet, we sprinkle glitter all over the boots. We set them aside to dry and wait for tomorrow. There they sit, on a shelf with a stained old tarp that rolls down over them for protection from dust and barn stuff. A rainbow of sparkly boots waits for their coming out party.

Jessica and Lea quickly help us clean up, then dash outside to the other barn to pet the horses. They ask Sam if they can go for a ride and he tells "Of course you can, and when you come back you need to feed the horses some oats, and don't forget to brush them. When you go for your ride, a few of us boys will ride with you. Fair enough?"

Sam's ex-partner Ray arrives with his two sons, Archie and Cody. Both boys are sturdy, blonde and handsome. They each have wide set eyes and look like burly movie stars. We are introduced, I look over to the girls, both girls blush. Oh no!

Lunch, is prepared by the Mexican cooks, Carmelita and Ramona, who Sam says have been here since they were kids. They also help with the cleaning and are part of the family. When lunch comes to a close, Dana Bea, Coach, Jessie, Lea, Sam, his buddy Ray and Ray's sons Cody and Archie all head out for a long ride: galloping and dodging tumbleweeds that fly and roll through the air. I stay back with Charlie. We begin to decorate bird houses, with the help of the grounds keeper Hector.

When everyone is accounted for with no news of anyone falling off a galloping horse, we settle in for dinner at a huge table in the big house. Conversations are light and the laughter contagious. I do notice that Archie always manages to sit next to Jessie and Cody by Lea. This is curious observation, and I make note. When all the kids head to the bunk house I feel the safety net I have around Jessica's waist beginning to stretch to its snapping point. To address this issue would insult the boy's father Ray, so I say nothing, just watch. With a deep breath I assume his sons have been raised well, and know how to treat and respect women.

Sam takes my hand under the table, squeezes it and says, "Enjoy your dessert Mama Bear."

Charlie is put to bed by his mother, so she and Coach can take a walk around the ranch. They sit on an old wagon that has been cleaned and spiffed up for tomorrow. Coach takes the reins and clicks his tongue in cheek. I hear Dana Bea giggling, when he yells, "Yaawh!" and hits the air with the reins. I back away from the window and let them ride off into the sunset, in their minds.

CHAPTER ELEVEN

This is the first time I hear the birds, their song is beautiful. I'll always remember this particular night we spend on the ranch. Sam had mentioned to me on the first day we arrived, "The birds that sing to you are called Meadowlarks. Not many people ever see them, but you can always hear their song."

Sam takes me by the hand and we go to the front of the farm house. Lazily we curl up in the swing under a tree and we rock. Neither of us is nervous or tired. It is just another evening with my best friend talking about dreams, kids, food, life and plans for the future. We ponder the evident question. Do we continue living next door to each other, or do we pool our money and buy a small house?

In the moonlight he still looks smug, and with this look comes a crooked smile. He looks at me and says, "We need to talk." His demeanor startles me, because he is out of character. He begins with the family here at the ranch, the people we are staying with, who take such good care of us.

"Nettie, the people you refer to as the owners are not the real owners."

I gasp, "Oh my Lord Sam, are we poaching on someone else's property?"

Sam holds my hand tight and informs me that the people I refer to as the owners are caretakers and he is the owner. I belt out a laugh, put my hand over my mouth and almost explode with hysterics and tell him, "You just never stop with the jokes, *Mr. Tan Hands.* You are too funny." I toss my head back and giggle a bit, but there is dead silence between us.

He calmly responds, "I'm not jokin' with you darlin'."

Softly, like a child I ask, "Sam, what exactly are you saying?" He tells me he inherited this ranch from his father who got it from his father and his before. "I was born and raised on this land. I was married at a young age, we had a son, then I studied, took classes and jumped through the hoops to became a Ranger. We had to move to a more populated area. The marriage broke up due to us being too young and stupid. She raised our son in Corpus Christi, and I went from city to city hunting down thugs, robbers, smugglers and as many other bad guys as I could find, to put them in jail. When I got shot in the shoulder and hand, unable to shoot with my right hand anymore, I came back to the ranch and the healing process began, along with depression."

Nonchalantly I ask, "Sam, just how much land do you have. I mean, how big is this ranch?"

He responds with, "It is always impolite to ask a rancher this question. Let's just say, it's not a Ranchette."

I apologize and confess to not knowing the rules of the Lone Star state. He grins and goes on to tell me the rest of the story, how he was shot and forced into early retirement.

I naturally ask about his son and want to know if he is in touch with him and the last time they had contact. Sam looks very sad and says that it has been a very long time. Too long.

"It was a difficult transition, being disabled for life, unable to shoot with accuracy, taking an early retirement from work in a field I loved. I am thankful I was not killed in action, but still, being disabled is not an easy road to go down. Years later I began to get restless and

CHAPTER ELEVEN

when my other former partner Hansen moved to the California coast, that's when I decided to follow him and move out West."

I interrupt, "Let me get this clear in my head, "In your career, you had two partners."

Sam proudly answers, "Correct, Ray and Hansen, two best men on the planet."

"I'm thankful I did go the West Coast, because I met the love of my life."

"Oh Sam, seriously is all of this true or are you kidding me again?"

He asks "Would you like to move back here after Jessie is out of high school, or college? Think about my proposal, so we can decide which direction to go." He repeats.

Of course I knew I could never leave my daughter and Little Charlie. I tell him, "I'll have to really sit on this one, and by the way cowboy, thanks for the jitters the night before our wedding. Does the hired help supply the guests with sleeping pills?"

He lets out a cackle. "Go ask Hector."

The sun is up and the cooks are back in the kitchen. The house smells of bacon, ham, biscuits, gravy and there is much chatter mixed with the sounds of dishes being moved about. I am still in shock from Sam's confession, but manage to get to the steaming pot and pour myself a cup of black coffee. I see Dana Bea curled up on the sofa with her coffee while Coach is outside chasing Charlie into the barn where the chickens live. My daughter looks a little peaked; I hope she is not coming down with something.

Dana Bea takes one look at me and observes, "Well don't you look like the cat who ate the mouse, what's up?"

"Yes dear, besides my wedding day?" Warmly patting her hand, we sip coffee, and I say nothing as promised. Oh boy, this is certainly going to be a game changer as Coach would say, especially in my relationship with my daughter.

The wedding is at sunset. We will have most of the day to relax. We girls gather and put our fancy center pieces on the tables. The Mexicans have been cooking for a week and have a pig underground on coals, wrapped with herbs, and it smells delicious. They are busy cooking carnitas, homemade tamales, enchiladas, rice, black beans, chips, guacamole, and fresh homemade corn tortillas. A side of beef also smolders underground. The sisters, Carmelita, Ramona and Marie along with their mother Lupe focus on the many dishes they prepare. They speak to each other in Spanish and happily work together. Kitchen sounds are of preparations, amazing smells, and joyful chatter. A true sense of love and family.

Before leaving the room, I turn back and wink at my daughter. She shrugs her shoulders and we both know what this means; we don't have to cook or do dishes. We exchange smiles.

CHAPTER TWELVE

Cowgirl Up

Ascending the staircase, I plan to take advantage of the perks that come with this wonderful stately house. I lay back and soak my body in a claw foot tub.

After my soak, I trot down the stairs, take Dana Bea by the arm and pull her up to our room. I fill the tub with warm bubbles and tell her to enjoy herself. I lay down and take a nap. I have no idea how long my daughter soaks, maybe she's still in there.

I descend the staircase to look for Jessie. I spot her with Archie, deep in conversation. They straddle a bale of hay to face each other. I wonder if he is asking her to marry him, or to run off into the night. Lea comes up to the house to be with Cody. Ok, they've paired off. Now I will have to police both girls, instead of focusing on my groom. I tell Dana Bea my concerns and she tells me to calm down, "Enjoy the day, your day, and give Jessica the respect she deserves. Archie too."

CHAPTER TWELVE

"I sigh deeply, okay dear, let's finish the floral arrangements."

Dana says, "Okay Mom," then takes me by the hand.

Jessie and Lea eat breakfast, then join us in the barn to have a girl fest and work our magic. We get the flowers out of the extra cold meat locker, cut the stems then wrap the stems with wet cloths. Now to place the flowers into each boot. We are feeling artistic and the girls feel the excitement and love being part of this special day. The tables are placed in a crooked line so guests can intermingle. We place the boots with overflowing bouquets back into cold storage.

Jessica, Lea, Archie and Cody take off again, they ride towards the end of the earth. I swallow hard, watch and let them go.

Dana Bea loves to ride the Appaloosa named Bean, and Coach likes the Quarter horse named Huddy. They enjoy rides alone, especially before sunset.

Seems Jessie has picked and she is already attached to her favorite horse; A paint called Gem. Sam tells Jessie not to worry, "These horses will always wait here for you to come back."

Dana Bea and Coach take Charlie for a ride in the old wooden wagon. The same wagon these two sat on last night. "It's a lot harder with horses." Sam joyfully teases Coach. Sam and his pals get the horses harnessed, and off they go, bouncing into the badlands.

"Sam has placed all of us into a western movie!" I say to whomever might be in ear shot.

The kids return from their outing and not a minute too soon. The helpers place lace table cloths on the long tables, and wait for the decorations. The boys put the horses away, the girls help too. They learn the chores that come with riding horses.

Then the girls run into the barn to help. They pull out the boots with flowers. They arrange the colorful boots along in a line down the center of the wedding party's long table. Everyone is gone, the house is quiet, the girls dash back to the bunk house to get cleaned up and dress. Dana Bea struggles to get Charlie bathed and ready. I am upstairs moving from side to side to encourage my hips to wiggle into my dress.

I slip on a loose fitting housecoat to conceal my wedding attire. With my daughter close by, we walk to the barn and wait. I hear a sound I am not prepared for, and once again surprised by Sam and his ideas.

Jessie and Lea jump into the shower and barely have enough time to toss on their sun dresses. Both girls pull their wavy hair back into a low ponytail.

Jessie runs into the barn to help out, wearing her new cotton sundress with orange and red designs. Her dress has the same pattern as her Aunt Dana Bea's, and both happily wear their new boots. Jessica adds a cream colored shawl she wraps around her shoulders to not expose the scars on her back and arms. Lea sits at her reserved table with Cody and Archie. Dana Bea is ready to step out, she looks stunning in her new colorful sun dress. Coach has worn out his son Charlie who sits quietly on a bale of hay, chewing a biscuit.

I peek out to investigate the sounds and see the Mariachi's who are grouping together to tune up their instruments. This is the sound

CHAPTER TWELVE

I heard a few minutes ago. They begin to play the most beautiful and authentic Mexican music. The sun begins to set, the sky is pink and orange, and the wind arrives with the sunset, which encourages the tumbleweeds to roll along.

Music fills the air as guests arrive in their finest Texas attire. When I peek out again I am stunned by the number of guests. I invited no one from my side because we are all here; this is my side. Sam said he was inviting a few of his Texas Ranger pals to the wedding.

Now, the lawn is packed with worn leather faces, tan hands and flashy wives. I also see our friends from California who Sam secretly flew in to attend our wedding, Hansen and his wonderful wife Connie. I feel nervous. There are some old folks, friends and neighbors from miles away. The guy from the hardware store is out there, and the lady from the florist shop too. I look towards Dana Bea with panic across my face. She peeks out the tiny window, looks through the cobwebs and exclaims, "Wow Sam, seriously!"

A lightweight robe still hides my dress, and the music begins, it is a Mexican version of the wedding march. Charlie, in a gray pin stripped suit and his new gray shiny boots jumps off the bale of hay and is ready for his part.

He wears a red bow tie, and says, "Hi Grandma." as he skids into home plate. I dust off the biscuit crumbs and pat the dust off his rump.

I walk back to the girls and slowly slip off my robe. The girls shriek in unison, I smile, reach up to touch my hair, then fan my armpits.

Charlie walks out of the barn holding a pillow with two rings on top. Following Charlie is my flower girl Jessica. She stops, looks back to me, flashes a big smile and whispers that her butt muscles are killing her from riding all day. I give her a nudge and push her out the barn door. She giggles with each step. Jessica drops pedals of yellow roses along the way. My dear Dana Bea looks back at me too, and softly asks if I'm ready, I smile and take her arm. There she is, so tall and confident, in her floral dress that flows with the breeze, she guides me along as we walk arm in arm towards Sam.

We step out of the shadow of the oak tree and see Sam. "Oh my heart, it pounds so loud, can everyone hear it?"

Sam waits, in his black pin striped suit, a white shirt with large white starched cuffs, and a leather bolo tie with a silver long-horn at the top where it is cinched up under his collar. I notice his polished black boots with silver tips on the toes. He wears his grandfather's shiny silver spurs for good luck. His white hair glistens against the sunset, and I notice he took the time to slick his hair back, I am weak in the knees.

With Dana Bea I walk in my tight red silk dress towards Sam. Holding a bouquet of yellow roses, and matching red high heels. *Yes, daughter dear, my shoes match.* I left my red boots in my room for a life that awaits. My long gray hair is pulled back into curls, and I can feel a few escape and tickle my neck. Dana Bea helps to capture my curls.

I step closer to the next chapter of my life and have no other thoughts except the pure luck of finding Sam. He waits and smiles as I move nearer. I look at my two girls and feel I am the luckiest person in the world.

I finally reach Sam. He takes my hands and the music stops. Charlie stands close to his Grandpa and my girls look smashing and bright, just like a spring bouquet.

CHAPTER TWELVE

The preacher talks of love, recites an Indian poem, then Sam and I look at each other, and I am thoroughly prepared for us to recite our vows as rehearsed, but ol' Sam, the forever spokesperson spouts out to the crowd, "It's been a hell of a courtship darlin'."

His outburst throws me off, but quickly I regain my composure, swallow hard and reply, "And it's not over yet, not by a long shot you long legged Texan."

I have no idea why I blurt out these words, it is so unlike me. I hear an applause and some whoops from the crowd, and snickers from the girls.

One of his friend's yells, "Hey Samuel, where you takin' your bride on your honeymoon?"

"Oh hell Clyde, we've been on a honeymoon since we met." and he gets more applause and cheers.

I stand next to him and try not to look like a harlot he picked up at the dime store. Sam laughs and we say our I dos, then kiss. He bends me over backwards and lays one on me in front of my kids, grandson and strangers. When we raise up, Sam speaks into the microphone and says to everyone, "I am proud to introduce to you to my darlin' companion, my wife and best friend Bertha." I gasp and try to hide my shocked face. I hear Dana Bea who lets out a cackle laugh like a drunken sailor, and Jessie asks her loudly, "Is that her real name?"

I glare into his eyes, while he clutches my hands, for his own protection. I squeeze real hard and dig my nails into his palms. He relinquishes my hands and we give each other a nice loving hug.

"You just wait until I get you alone buster." I whisper He doesn't even say one word. He picks me up into his big arms and twirls me around in circles. I let out a young girl's scream and try to keep my ankles together and not show the guests more than they bargained for.

The party begins, the Mariachi troupe picks up their instruments, and plays. We take photos and make sure everyone at the tables have access to disposable cameras. No need to keep the guests waiting for a professional photographer. We figure, if anyone gets a good picture of us, then great.

We stop to look at each other, pose, kiss and hug. Sam takes me by the hand and leads me to a bench that circles the huge oak tree. He kisses my neck and whispers, "Nice dress." I smile back and tell him I am full of surprises. He says he has a gift hidden back at the table, he melts my heart and I am like a young bride, blushing and in love. Our alone time is short but necessary. We walk back to the head table to open my gift. I wonder, "Now what has he done?"

I open the box and beneath the tissue paper I see a crystal ball, a paperweight made out of hand blown glass with a design inside of two dolphins in an embrace. Only the two of us know the significance of this gift. Then I reach under the table and bring out and surprise him with my gift. He smiles with that twinkle in his eye and carefully, and much slower than I and much more meticulous with the wrapping paper, slowly opens the box. The lid comes off and he peers inside and looks at a silver sculpture of two dolphins on a piece of polished driftwood. We laugh and hear loud clapping, whistles and cat calls. I can tell this reception is going to be a wild one.

He and I sit at the long table that Hector had crafted and look at the amazing foods set before us.

CHAPTER TWELVE

Shock runs through me when my shy daughter Dana Bea stands up and clinks the side of her glass a few times using the side of her fork, ping, ping, ping. Once she has everyone's attention, she acknowledges the crowd of strangers.

"I'll never forget the first time I laid eyes on my mother and Sam together. I was standing on the balcony above the beach, when I spot them. They were standing in the ocean up to their knees, she in a long cotton dress, he in a Hawaiian shirt and shorts. Then this stranger bends down, picks up my mother and begins to twirl her up into the air like pizza dough. The guests howl. I thought Mother would scream for help and I was ready to jump off the deck and come to her aid when she jumps on Sam's back and rides him like that black stallion over there by the fence. She rides him out of the shallow water, and kicks his hips then runs him out onto the sandy beach." Dana Bea finishes, smiles and sits down.

The guests go crazy with her story, they yell and whoop, while I sit mortified with my hand over my mouth. She got me today, so did Sam who laughs and beams from the memory, mostly from being exposed as a predator! I decide not to try to outdo her story, or his and instead, I stand up and take a bow. Jessica is laughing too and Lea gets a kick out of these stories. Dana Bea looks at me and winks, Coach smacks his thigh with his hand and laughs while Charlie is knee deep in Mexican food. Coach, overwhelmed with joy kisses my daughter on the cheek.

Dinner is an event all by itself we could have grazed all night, just like the cattle. Everyone is happy and one by one retired Rangers come up to tell me about the great guy I married. Some talk about their close calls they encountered as active Rangers. Some stories are about how Sam saved their life. Each and every one has a story, and the wives walk up one by one to wish us well.

I let the kids go off after dinner and ask that they please return when the music begins. Archie is Jessica's first crush, and he seems like a very nice young man.

"Go, have fun, enjoy. But don't go too far. We have dancing and the cake cutting." The four kids wave and dash off into the night.

We party well into the night. It all begins after dinner when the blue grass band gets set up on a flatbed truck. Their opening number is called, *Anders Corner*. Sam leans over and tells me the name of each song and who made it famous and the year is was popular. This one is called *Foggy Mountain Breakdown*. I love it so much and also love to watch these old timers play. The music fills the night air and everyone seems to know how to dance to these sounds except me and my family. *Blue Moon of Kentucky* is a great number, and the female vocalist really belts it out. The music seems to go on forever, and I have never in my life danced to this type of music. Sam takes my hand, and leads me to the dance floor. All I can do is apologize for stepping on his shiny boots before we even begin. He whispers some simple instructions, and tells me he will teach me to do the Texas two-step. "If you get confused, or mixed up, just follow my lead and my arms will let you know which direction to turn." Sam says, "Okay, let's go darlin'. Two to the right, one to the left, repeat, two to the right, one to the left. Oh, and you do these steps backward. I do the opposite leading, but I go forward."

This doesn't seem fair one bit, but it seems to work. Ready, and off we go into the crowd, circling round and round the dance floor. He then takes Coach and Dana Bea off to the side, and in a few whispers off they go, melting into the crowd of dancers to a song called *Salty Dog Blues*. Jessica and Archie return and they hit the dance floor too. I watch Archie as he instructs her; she listens and looks so happy.

CHAPTER TWELVE

Then off they go, round and round on the dance floor. Everyone swirls around the floor in a wide circle. Lea and Cody finally arrive. A bunch of retired weathered-face Rangers in their finest cowboy hats, and their wives with big hair take off and dance around the dance floor in a large circle. The kids dance too; Charlie, dances and twirls in circles with his arms outstretched, as free as a bird.

I finally meet Ray's wife, Peg. She is dramatic, her hair is fluffy with perfectly organized gray curls, one side she tucks behind her ear. She is a natural sexy lady. I can't help but notice her extra-large south western style jewelry. I instantly like her. She is friendly but guarded. I can tell, if she is your friend, she will be a friend for life. I also sense that no one messes with her, or her sons. It is obvious why her boys are handsome and I sense she rules the roost over Ray.

Even though Dana Bea gave a speech, and ate, and danced, she still doesn't seem to be her spunky self. In all of my happiness, I focus on my daughter.

Later, as the crowd of well-wishers begin to thin out, Sam asks me if I'd like to jump in his jeep and head to a town, find a place close by and spend the night.

I look up at him, snuggle in nice and close, look up into the face I love, and tell him my true feelings. "Life is short Sam. Let's stay here with our family, and be here for breakfast."

He responds with, "Damn woman, I was hopin' you'd say that." He picks me up and gives me a nice twirling hug. Boy this man surely loves to twirl me around in circles; He lets out a whoop.

Feeling the need to rest I excuse myself to sit on the veranda. Our time here at the ranch is coming to an end and as I look around at the barns, cattle, horses, corn fields, I recall all the fun the kids have had and I know I have to make a decision.

I wonder if life would be easier if we lived in Texas, away from watchful eyes of the law in Northern California.

I wonder if any of the wedding guests thinks, "She surely doesn't look like a kidnapper."

I look towards Jessie, as she learns how to saddle a horse with the help of Archie and think, no one would ever expect she is not my granddaughter. We have made it, we have blended in. She is almost of legal age. Jessica is growing up, and her once curly hair is now long, thick and wavy. She is a pretty girl and my heart jumps for joy when I look at her face—what a blessing.

If I turn myself in and get this over with, I suppose I would do jail time, but she would never have to go back to her low-life, drunken parents. I think of all these things as I sit on the veranda alone, listening to the birds along the fences, happy and free.

Thoughts pass through my mind as I sit and contemplate a life, here, on the ranch. Just then, one of the older wives sneaks up behind me and with a singing voice chirps, "I know what you are thinkin'."

I make a half turn, smile and reply, "Oh, you do?"

"Now, don't you go worrying about your age or about Sam. I can tell he loves you."

CHAPTER TWELVE

I don't reply, only wonder who she is, and where in the world she has pulled this malarkey out of—her butt? I am tired, worried and have to make a huge decision in my life. I don't know this person, and feel she is only making small talk to get information. I sense an air of gossip and negativity surrounding her. She waits for a response. I abruptly stand and excuse myself saying, "Well, off to my family. Our visit on my private veranda is over."

The next morning, Sam waves from across the parking area next to the barn. I see Dana Bea and Charlie in with the chickens collecting morning eggs. It's all too perfect, too normal and innocent. Maybe I need to lay down my paranoia, celebrate my girl Jessica and pat myself on the back. No, I don't dare lay down my sword. I must stay alert. This journey is not over, not just yet.

Our entire family heads to the city for some sightseeing in Dallas. This day should have been our honeymoon day. We chose to be with family and we are so happy we did. We visit the building where Lee Harvey Oswald shot President Kennedy. Next, feeling solemn, we stop for coffee and sodas in downtown Dallas. We look at statues and stately old buildings but feel sad for our country and Jackie Kennedy. We find a place to eat, then return back to the ranch and prepare to pack, rest and fly home the next day.

Day ten arrives, we return to the airport. We gang of Californians are all on the same flight. Dana Bea looks haggard and tired. Jessica seems sad and says a long good bye to Archie, who engulfed her in a sweet embrace. They exchanged addresses and phone numbers. Oh dear me. Jessica likes Archie just as much as Lea likes Cody. Once on the plane, these best friends snuggle into their seats to whisper and giggle back and forth, constantly interrupting each other's story. Thankfully, Charlie sleeps most of the way.

Two weeks after we return, Dana Bea discovers she is going to have another baby. This news explains a lot, mainly about her low energy.

Jessica and Lea are back to earth and continue to watch the muscle boys on the beach who play volley ball, but both girls left their hearts in Texas. It is a gloomy time.

CHAPTER THIRTEEN

The File

Jessica and I sit on our patio; she informs me it is high time I tell her the story of her life. The story of how she became my granddaughter. I wish it was that sweet and simple. She sits with eager anticipation and innocent eyes and a smile. A young girl on the threshold of womanhood. I tell her I'll be right back then go back inside our duplex to fetch the file from under the bed.

Sam leaves to spend the day with his buddy Hansen. I am left alone with Jessie, who waits. Dana Bea patiently waits for a phone call about our inevitable conversation.

I make us some hot mint tea; we sit down outside on the deck. I begin with my life in Northern California. I tell her about losing my husband to a heart attack. I tell her about my dog Buddy, a Golden Retriever. I tell her about my sister Abigale.

Jessica chimes in and respectfully says, "Nettie, today is about me, now get to the point, I know all about your life with Jim and Abby."

CHAPTER THIRTEEN

She has my number and steers me right into the dark side, unknowingly and unprepared for the truth. The file is on the table between us. I will tell her the ugly truth, hold her hands across the small table and go into great detail, maybe too much. The file opens, to reveal the photos.

"For you Jessie Dear." I wait.

When I was living alone I heard you cry almost every night. Your screams filled the night air. You were barely two years old. You lived around the corner from my house. Dana Bea came up to visit, and we listened to your wails of pain as she and I visited inside my home. Your aunt and I walked around the block to investigate these terrible pitiful sounds.

I tell her about seeing her *dad* smoking a cigarette and watching us. I tell her about the window without glass. I look into her eyes and tell her about the little girl standing in the window staring back at me.

"It was you Jessie." She begins to tear up and large droplets fall to the table. Her tears travel down her face as I forge along. If I stop, I will never be able to tell her what she needs and deserves to hear.

"Jessica, a few weeks pass by, and one evening when I step outside onto my porch, I see something move, something under my Dogwood tree next to the porch steps. I am cold, and see something glowing across the street, in the grouping of pine trees. It was your dad, smoking and watching. He had a stick and slapped his palm over and over." Jessica wipes her eyes with a hankie on the table. "Jessie, he walked up to my curb and asked if I had seen you."

THE FILE

Now comes the hard part. I must tell her. I clear my throat and tell her the story of her becoming my granddaughter.

"Jessie, I found you on a biting cold evening, curled up on your knees in a fresh layer of snow. I carefully stepped down on to the white carpet, bent over and picked you up. You quickly curled up into my robe and I carried you up my stairs and into my home. Then we lay by the fire."

Jessie stares out towards the ocean taking it all in. I wait, give her a minute to digest. She turns back and asks me if I stole her from her parents.

I answer her with honesty. "Yes I did Jessica, and I would do it all again if I had to make the same decision."

She turns back to view the waves to absorb this information she desperately craves.

She studies the photos, the wounds, the scars, her matted hair, bruises on her legs, buttocks and the open wounds on her face. Her swollen black and blue eye. She holds each photo and takes in each one. She looks closely and asks for my magnifying glass. I dash inside and quickly retrieve it. She puts her eye to each polaroid photo and studies her wounds. I sit and wipe my eyes and feel so much love and sorrow for her I want to die. She sets the file down, wipes her eyes, looks towards me and says, "I remember the hurt." Astonished, I listen.

She calmly, with a soft voice says, "I remember crying, I remember the sharp pain and his voice, but I have no recall of my mother, do I have one?" She innocently asks.

"Yes Jessie, you have a mother."

CHAPTER THIRTEEN

She swallows hard and wipes her flow of tears then sets the hankie down on the table, looks at me and says, "Thank you Grandma."

"No, Jessica, it is I who should thank you, for coming into my life."

She adds, "It must have been worse to take these photos than to show them."

Unable to speak, I nod yes.

"Why did he beat me, what could I have done to make him so angry?" She quietly asks. She looks back out to the ocean and asks, "Why didn't my mother help me, why didn't she stop him, where was she, is she my real mom, is he my real dad?" Her questions flow.

"Jessica, let's take this one step at a time. When you are ready there are very capable people to help get your answers. If you want, we can have a DNA test done on both your parents. One thing at a time my Dear."

Jessie stands up and walks around the small table and puts her young fresh young arms around my neck and buries her face into my hair.

I feel her warm breath on my ear and neck. She whispers, "Grandma, you always smell like lavender and cooking flour." This description makes us laugh.

She asks me if her parents searched for her. "Well, now Jessie, that is a loaded question." I proceed to tell her about the lack of information on the television and radio, after I took her.

THE FILE

Nonchalantly I mention the county fair, but before I can get to the part about seeing her drunken father she interrupts with childlike excitement. "I totally remember you taking me to the fair, I remember the sheep and all the lights."

Omitting the part about her parents being stumbling drunk or about us running for safety, seemed like a logical decision. She is thrilled to regain a childhood memory of her evening at the fair.

I misjudged Jessie, she is not a weak person and our conversation is not over by a long shot. She takes a bite of cookie, and her last sip of tea and announces. "I'm going to find him, and my mother too. I have a few things I need to say to them."

I witness a deep seated anger bubbling up from the depths of her soul. I agree to back her financially and offer Sam's services in the search. She retreats back to her little alcove, and curls up into a ball. I quietly put the cups away and wash the cookie plate. I think to myself, somewhere along this journey Jessica went from calling me Nettie to Grandma. Either one is fine with me. I love it, her voice saying Grandma makes my heart dance.

This is an excruciating day but now her story is finally out, and filleted wide open for her to study and do what she needs to do to heal.

Jessie and Lea decide they need a new look, a more adult look. They feel the need to express themselves artistically. They are old enough to change their look, but I believe they actually heard this on a local television advertisement, because I heard it too, but didn't change my look.

CHAPTER THIRTEEN

Later in the day, Jessica and Lea knock and peek in, I am speechless. Lea's hair is just below her jawbone and she has some blonde streaks around her face. It looks very cute and sure enough, she looks older. I respond with the only phrase I can think of, "Where is Lea?" I ask.

She loves hearing this and giggles. "Cute, huh Nettie, I can tuck it behind my ears and wear head bands if I want."

Then Jessie pops her head into the room. I gasp, her waist length hair is cut to the bottom of her ear lobes. She has a long side bang, cut to the earlobe also.

"Oh, Jessie, you look very European." I lie through my teeth. She loves this observation. Jessie informs me that the hairdresser braided her hair at the base of her neck, then she cut it off above the rubber band.

"Grandma, I had thirteen inches of hair taken off and you only need ten inches to be able to mail your hair to the Locks of Love Foundation."

Feeling two generations removed, I listen while she explains. It is an organization that collects long natural hair, then they make wigs for anyone who has to undergo Chemotherapy. Locks of Love is affiliated with the American Cancer Society.

"Oh, wonderful thought, I'm so proud of you girls." The girls giggle and sweep their heads around from side to side, jokingly I caution them not to do that move on the deck, you might toss yourselves over the rail.

THE FILE

"Did you both send your hair into Locks of Love?"

Lea answers, "No, well I thought about it, but I kept changing my mind on the length, then when I finally said to take more off, she measured it and I didn't have the required ten inches to send. I am so bummed."

I push their buttons and add, "I hope the boys in Texas like your new look."

They scream.

CHAPTER FOURTEEN

The Lone Star State

SAM COMES HOME WITH A HUGE PIZZA IN A BOX. He is so smart. We eat together and the room is very tense. You can feel it in the air, Jessica's hostility has begun to brew, but not towards us. Her anger is directed to the man who beat her and to her mother who failed to step up.

When we first returned from Dallas, Sam and I agreed we should move back to his ranch and make Texas our home. I did a lot of soul searching because of my lovely daughter with another baby on the way, and my active grandson. These elements made my decision extremely difficult.

After Jessie graduated from Steps she enrolled at San Luis Obispo High School. We decide the time will be right for us to move, as soon as she graduates. She is in her last year and we begin to make arrangements.

Sam notifies Hector, then flies back to measure and prepare for renovations and expansion. While this is going on, we also have arranged a search party to locate the whereabouts of Jessica's parents. Ranger Sam and Ranger Hanson are hot on their trail.

CHAPTER FOURTEEN

Sam assures Jessica, "It's okay, life always comes around full circle."

"We must take care of business and not hide in Texas," he assures me.

Sam makes some phone calls and the wheels of justice begin to move forward. Yes, I could be arrested. There is also the brutal fact that she may never find them. There are so many facets and this search could go in several directions. I keep telling myself, "It's all okay, it's out of our hands. It's time."

Sam has a long talk with Jessica and unfortunately this chat is private.

Lea and Jessica walk across the stage to receive their diplomas. They move their tassels then toss their caps. It's a joyous day, and their next step is college.

In the meantime, Coach receives a pink slip. This notice is from his school district. Many other counties in the state of California are making budget cuts. The biggest hit for public schools are the charter schools sprouting up. Some counties have very low funds to keep teachers employed full time. He is offered a part time coaching position. Coach knew of the rumors and felt his number might come up. Still, it is a financial worry. He tries not to upset his pregnant wife. He asks for time to gather his thoughts about part time work, which also means no health benefits.

I feel guilty for enrolling Jessica into Steps. I would have happily enrolled her into our local public school, but our case had *special circumstances*. Finally, I did let her attend the public high school and Lea joined her. I now know how important it is to support the local school system.

Dana Bea goes into labor and I can't imagine how stressful this is for her as her husband searches for work. Fortunately, his health insurance coverage will be active for several months, and thankfully they are still covered for the birth and hospital stay and care. But one day his insurance and unemployment checks will end. Realization hangs over their heads.

If Sam is to continue searching for Jessie's parents he needs a cover story. We need to decide who Sam is, exactly. If the police ask why is this man, Sam, helping Jessica. Who pays him? Where has this child been for the past seventeen years? Where is she now? Who raised her?

Hansen takes the lead in the search because he has no traceable connection to me and Hansen has all the answers, plus a leather lined face to scare away the worse convict.

Sam and Hansen do their part for Jessica, and together they search. These two former Texas Rangers finally locate her father, Richard Clute, in prison.

"Shocking." I comment.

I don't share this information with my daughter. She does not need the stress. I keep it to myself for now and listen to Sam.

He is incarcerated in a State prison called Pelican Bay, located in Northern California, close to the Oregon border which seems to be located close to a bay. Sam schedules to meet with the warden, and tells Jessie the news. She balks, isn't ready, she confesses she is scared and frightened. She wants to meet him, but she is afraid of him and

CHAPTER FOURTEEN

his reaction. She is afraid he will lash out at her, hurt her. Jessica pleads her case and says she needs more time to prepare mentally. Sam agrees with her, the decision is her call, her journey, and no one intends to put any pressure on her.

Dana Bea gives birth to a dark haired baby girl she names Abigale Lane. My world stops, when I hear my sister's name and my daughter's maiden name put together. Engulfed with joy for the gift my daughter gives me, a beautiful granddaughter. She calls her infant Abby. She is snuggly and happy. She cuddles, coos and Dana Bea puts her daughter in a tight wrap to swaddle her, using a soft blanket to give her baby girl security. She shows Jessica how to do this while Jessie goes over to help. Dana shows Lea and Jessica how to swaddle and explains why this is important, in case one of the girls has to babysit.

Hansen drives to the Prison to check out the situation and talk to the warden. I thought Sam was working on the house, while back in Texas, but he was not. He phones his former Ranger pals, who are looking into any positions that are opening up for a teaching position and in need of a coach, preferably close to the Dallas area.

When Hansen drives off to meet the warden, I am not sure if I should bake more cookies, hold Jessica in my arms, or cook meals for my daughter and her family. But what I really have a desire to do is go to Pelican Bay with Hansen and spit in Jessie's father's face.

New mother and little Abby are doing very well, and Coach is a rock. He plays with Charlie, keeps him busy and quiet, and he also cooks. He and his son play outside, drive to parks and playgrounds. He seems resolved to be out of work for the moment. I take over three days' worth of food. Pack food into containers with morning foods, and casseroles. Jessie stops by to help too. My visit is short, just enough time to deliver, scoop up my granddaughter, rock her, and look at her new tiny face. Then I leave my daughter alone to heal, regain her strength and become one with her daughter Abigale.

Back home I focus on Jessie. She has a level head and does not want to prejudge or make plans or imagine a wonderful meeting. I caution her not to go inside the prison with negative feelings. She is in a holding pattern and spends most of her time with her aunt.

CHAPTER FIFTEEN

Changes

Hansen returns from Northern California with news of Rich, who is not aware of Hansen's visit. The warden gives permission for Jessica to visit her father. They will talk using a phone, with thick glass between them. She is ready, but disappointed to be separated, and relieved at the same time. She tells Hansen she will decide who to travel with after Sam comes back. Sam will comfort her and guide her before she goes inside the prison to talk to this parasite.

I realize I must overcome my negativity and hatred for Rich, because it's not healthy.

Sam returns from Texas and says we need a family meeting. Oh for heaven's sake, I think to myself, can't our family just watch television and relax like normal families. Can't we just spend a weekend relaxing, and reading books. Jessica tells Lea she can't come over; we're having a private family meeting.

Lea's response is, "Seriously?"

CHAPTER FIFTEEN

Dana Bea packs up her baby, and maneuvers up the stairs, while Coach and Charlie follow protectively behind her. The family is together.

Sam clears his throat, then begins to say how sorry he with the news of Coach's position as a varsity coach dwindle to a part time position. Jessica is nervous and thinks this meeting is about her. Sam is a straight shooter and goes on to announce that there is an opening for a varsity coach in a town called Weatherford, not far from the ranch.

Dana and Coach both ask, "What?" Then in unison, "Texas?"

"Yep, Weatherford." Sam repeats.

It's about 60 miles from Dallas, but the good news is, the ranch is right in between.

Coach is dumbfounded and exclaims, "Texas?"

"Yes, Texas, clean out your ears." Sam jokes. He hands Coach a list with names and phone numbers. "Get on it boy, let's make it happen."

"My darlin' companion and I will be moving back to the ranch in another few months, as soon as the remodeling is complete, and it sure would be nice to have your family over for dinner."

Dana Bea softly asks, "Texas?"

"Yes darlin', Texas, don't you and Coach ever clean out your ears?" Sam smiles again with his witty come back, they stare dumbfounded. The rest of us bust up laughing, mostly from nervous energy.

CHANGES

Coach says, "Well, I guess we have a lot to talk about honey." He is afraid to ask any more questions, but not Dana Bea, who gets valuable information from Sam. He tells them to go on the web page and check it out. "Check out the posting for the job opening then call me." Dana Bea feels a sense of relief and interest in digging deeper into Sam's hare brain idea.

"There are two old timers who just retired, and man, this might be your lucky day Coach."

We chat for an hour or more, and all agree Sam can shock our company right into a trance. Dana Bea and Coach hug us, stand up and say, "Thanks," and walk out the door like zombies.

Sam stands at the door and shouts as they descend the stairs, "Weatherford is home to the Texas Rangers, check it out."

Two days later Coach rings up Sam, says he has been in contact with the hiring board and he has an interview this coming Monday. Assuming Sam says, "Great, I'll fly back with you."

Jessie and I move in with Dana Bea for a couple of days to help with Charlie, clean up and cook meals. Jessie helps most of the time keeping Charlie occupied, so Dana Bea can tend to little Abby. Life is as it should be, with one too many irons in the fire.

Jessie and Lea are both accepted and decide to attend Cal Poly in San Luis Obispo. This college is well known as an agriculture college with high ratings. The girls said they are not ready for a move far

CHAPTER FIFTEEN

away, and Lea's parents can't afford out of state tuition. The girls are thinking about renting an apartment. I have to jump in and toss out other possibilities. "How about you rent a room from Hansen and Connie. Both you girls have known them since you were very young and Jessie, you've spent many sleep overs there and feel safe and welcome."

I go on, "If you move into an apartment you both will have to get part time jobs. You will also need a car. Many things to consider girls."

They both look at each other with a wide-eyed look of, "*Should we drop the bomb?*" They ask me to sit down. I do, and in all innocence I am ill prepared for their speech. Jessica begins, "We have some exciting news, and we don't want this to be an issue, but, well, Nettie, Cody and Archie are going to attend Cal Poly as well." She continues to pad the story with many other euphemisms. Cal Poly is a well-known college for cattleman and agriculture, they think one or two years will add a perk to their resume if they attend this specific college, for their life's work on a ranch.

I can tell the girls have this all laid out and their speech has a practiced delivery. I struggle to not appear stunned, and calmly ask, "Where will the brothers live? And where will you girls live?"

This curve ball hits them right between the eyes, they stare back. They each swallow hard, "We are thinking of renting a four-bedroom house."

"Let me understand this proposal. You girls want to rent a house and share all costs with Ray's sons, while the four of you attend Cal Poly, correct?"

I have them on the hot burner and I wish for Sam to walk in, but he is still in Texas with Coach, which puts this squarely on my shoulders.

Shaking inside from a little anger and a lot of insults inferring I am so naïve, I take control and stay firm.

"Girls, I know all too well how much you like Archie and Cody." I totally understand the attraction, they are nice looking boys, smart polite boys. But to move in together, attend college, study together, do household chores, and be roommates is totally out of the question. I will talk to your Grandpa when he returns and see how he feels about this. I know he will talk to the boy's father and see how Ray feels about this arrangement. So let's not get your heart set on this plan just yet."

They mumble in agreement.

The girls quickly vanish into the other room where the new mother rests with her baby girl, Abby. Or so I thought, instead Dana Bea steps into the room holding her baby girl, sporting her signature reserved grin and asks, "Tea Nettie?"

"Oh Dana Bea, you little stinker, yes, thank you honey." She gets a wink.

I stew about the house sharing. I lay awake throughout the night, tossing and turning. Dana Bea's sheets look like I put an egg beater under the covers.

Sam phones just as I begin to doze off. He wants to tell me all about the remodel. "It is really cool lookin' darlin', I am so excited for you to put your finishing touches on our place."

He goes on, "The veranda is perfect, I can see us out there doing what we do best; talkin' and eatin' your zucchini bread." He happily jokes. He chuckles at himself for being so clever and silly.

CHAPTER FIFTEEN

I don't have the heart to tell Sam about Ray's boys. No need to disrupt his excitement. Once Sam returns home with Coach, everything will settle down. He and I will have a nice long chat.

All is well with the women in the house who are here to help Dana Bea. She is breast feeding Abby, and I am cooking for her when *Miss College Girl* wakes up. She reheats the bacon and scrambled eggs. I tell myself to stay calm, have an open mind and be a positive force. Dana Bea has her baby to her breast with a pink baby blanket over her.

She watches sleepy Jessie, looks at me, rolls her eyes and whispers, "Whatever."

With a subtle nod, I shrug my shoulders and pour myself a hot cup of coffee and bring in a cup of herbal tea for Dana Bea.

Tuesday the boys are home from the long trip. Sam sweeps me off my feet, Coach puts his hands on the sides of Dana Bea's face and give her a long kiss, Jessica runs back into her room.

Sam says we'll talk about the expansion and tile later.

Coach tells Dana Bea the interview went very well, and the tour around campus was an interesting concept. His hopes are high, but I can tell he doesn't want her to get her hopes up. He continues to downplay this process. But he can't stop talking about the pay, the team spirit, and adds, he will also be teaching one science class. This position is right up his alley and he is more than excited. He is worried because of the competition. They assure him they will call.

I can't take the stress any longer and suggest to Sam that we head home, sit and enjoy the view overlooking the rocks. We laugh at this

CHANGES

remark because we share a joke, "Our marriage is on the rocks." Again we laugh and hug but no one else seems to think it's funny. We leave yelling bye to Jessica, through her closed bedroom door. I step up to the door and tell her to get dressed and see if Aunt Dana Bea needs help.

Two weeks pass and no word from the high school in Weatherford. Then, late one morning the phone rings, it is the secretary from Weatherford High, not the principal. She asks to talk to Coach, Dana Bea carefully passes the phone. He sits down and speaks with quiet confidence. Dana Bea waits and watches Coach as he listens.

He replies, "I understand, yes, I do, yes I will, thank you." He hangs up the phone, drops his head, then cups his hands around his face. He sits there for a few minutes collecting his thoughts.

She questions, "Coach, honey, are you okay?"

He slowly looks up, then toward her and says in a low monotone voice, "We need to find a realtor in Weatherford."

Dana Bea phones us immediately and I can barely understand her speedy chatter because of the shouts coming from Sam, "Oh hell yeah Coach, hell yeah!"

The job begins soon, because he needs to be there in mid-summer to begin football practice. Sam calls him back and gives him a few names so he can find a place to stay. I tell Sam I can go back and help look with a realtor while Dana Bea tends to the kids. Jessica can stay and help also.

Off we go back to Texas. Coach will be spending time at the high school, while Sam and I look at homes. We know the price range and will learn about the best areas for housing.

CHAPTER FIFTEEN

Dana Bea is in shock and stays mum. Before we leave for Texas she confides into me, "My milk is going to dry up if our family doesn't settle down."

"Good grief my girl," and for the first time in a long while, we share a good laugh.

Sam tells her about the large lake for boating, sailing or swimming and cooling down, it's more than an hour's drive from your place, and everyone here says it is beautiful, it's called Lake Tawakoni, look it up. This is a perk as Texas can fry the fur off a coyote in mid-summer. A lake adventure will be a nice retreat. But it's a whole lot easier if you just buy a blow up swimming pool for the kids.

One month later, Coach is living in Texas in a motel, he is on the field every morning including Saturdays. The team has their first skirmish in a week. It is hot and dry. Coach is slowly acclimating to this shocking change of weather. Teaching in San Luis Obispo, with the coolness from the ocean just across a low mountain range, was as comfortable as teaching in a day spa. In Weatherford, beyond the high school, the principal and the kids, to his surprise he is beginning to enjoy the many things this town has to offer. He feels he's in a good place and looks forward to the coming games.

We look at six houses and so far only a few are nice. The realtor phones the next day saying a home just came on the market. She suggests we take a look. I am warned that the owner's personal belongings are still there, so I have to look beyond, imagine this home without their life still there, overlook the mess, their color choices and all of the things that confuse the buyer. We drive out to a small man-made lake named, The Lagoon. She turns a corner and pulls up to the curb on a street, High Sky.

CHANGES

We get out of the car, I see the house, a white stucco house with a red tile roof, Spanish style. There is a half wall in front which creates a private court yard with drought tolerant landscape.

I want to yell, "Yes, I'll take it."

Great price, great floor plan, but it needs paint and cleaning and some tile work, but all in all, what a great place! I phone my daughter and tell her the lay out, and details. Sam goes to the high school and tells Coach to make plans to see it this evening. By noon the next day they put in an offer. A low offer because of paint and cleaning. The sellers wait two days then accept. I tell Sam, "Dana Bea is going to flip out when she sees this jewel."

Sam states the obvious, "There's a good chance we'll sleep very well tonight darlin'."

We drive back to the ranch, eat great foods then sit outside and listen to the Meadowlarks as they get ready for darkness and quiet time. We literally flop on the bed, exhausted.

Next morning, I finally take a look at our own remodel and the tile Sam chose. We walk around with our hot coffee mugs and I am amazed at the changes. The arches, coves, a small private kitchen, and the patio is so perfect, with the large tree where we said our vows offering shade. He leads me to the bathroom and shows me a dusty box and cuts it open, there staring back at me are the most unique Spanish tiles I've ever seen. I tear up because of the beautiful and intricate Spanish design on these tiles.

I look up at Sam, put my arms around his waist and tell him, "You have an eye for the arts, you are a true artist."

CHAPTER FIFTEEN

He smiles that crooked smile and seems to blush and pulls me in close. I ask him what that narrow window is for, the one right next to where our bed sits. He explains his idea. "We will put two glass shelves in there to display the glass paperweight and the silver dolphins we gave to each other on our wedding day."

Flabbergasted with his thoughtfulness and foresight I tell him, "A perfect spot to catch morning light."

We mosey in for breakfast then take it outside. Ray stops by and when he parks his truck I get a lump in my throat. I still have failed to mention *the plan*, which includes his sons and college.

Ray walks up to us, says hello and sits down. Ramona brings him a cup of coffee. Sam says, "Mornin' Ray, what brings you out with the birds?" Sam obnoxiously chirps.

Ray says he wants to talk to us about the boys, and college. Sam looks bewildered and mentions, "Well, sure Ray, what's up?"

Ray tells Sam *the plan* and the men have quite a discussion about, morals, future mishaps, our friendship, and the kid's education. Ray doesn't know what to think. He has heard of Cal Poly, as California Polytechnic, and is impressed and excited for his sons. I stay quiet and listen.

We toss scenarios and possibilities around without mentioning the obvious. No one mentions pregnancy, or marriage, or breakups. We grandparents and parent talk over and around the kids, we scan the idea of college and skirt the issue of sex. Basically we win the contest for not mentioning the elephant in the room.

CHANGES

I finally speak up and ask Ray how he feels about his boys sharing a house with two girls. Sam is shaking his head no. He does not look happy. He asks me how I feel about it. With a deep breath I tell Ray, "It's like pouring honey on an ant hill."

He agrees and asks, "What can we do?"

They need housing, they need a car and they will date, *they will*. I suggest, that if they find a house with an extra room, maybe a *house mom* could live there and help out, cooking cleaning and keeping an eye out. The guys like this idea and we toss it and others around like a ping pong balls.

It's time to notify the girls, Jessica specifically. We will tell her about the conversation between the boys' father, her grandpa Sam and me.

Sam and I have a meeting concerning money. I phone Dana and make them an offer. They accept.

This is our solution, "I will loan Dana Bea and Coach the money for their down payment on their house in Weatherford, then you and Lea can rent Dana Bea's house.

She actually agrees to this and understands the importance of keeping them safely apart from the boys. I love her for this, and she said she'll phone Lea. Ray tells his sons to find an apartment close to campus.

"Jessie, if you go on a diet, it's a lot easier if you don't have a cupcake right under your nose."

"Oh grandma! That's just down right corny."

CHAPTER SIXTEEN

A Fathers Confession

SAM SUGGESTS WE TAKE A TRIP ACROSS TEXAS to a town called Waco. He says there is a museum he wants to show me. He is very excited and proud to be my private tour guide at the Museum of the Texas Rangers. I wonder privately if every town in the state of Texas has a Texas Ranger museum.

He corrects me and says I should not refer to them as ex-Rangers, and says, "Once a Ranger, always a Ranger, but at some point you become a former Ranger." I get it loud and clear, and feel like a chump.

Our family once again has a plan—another relocation plan. Jessie and Lea come over to help and lend a hand. We also need to enlighten them about our long range plans. The girls happily jump in to help with the kids as Dana Bea and I pack up her belongings. Dana Bea tells them she'll leave dishes and a couch that is not worth moving. I will buy the girls linens and towels and they will be all set. I don't mention the boys.

CHAPTER SIXTEEN

Archie and Cody enroll at California Polytechnic in San Luis Obispo. They will absorb much knowledge, graduate and then return to Texas to help out on the ranch with all of the political goings on about cattle, the drought, and the science of watering corn fields to produce feed for cattle. Today there is much more to know about ranch land management. With climate changes, and drought issues, it's not as lucrative as it once was. Sam looks forward to Cody and Archie's expertise, information and advice.

We pay drivers to deliver our cars to Texas. Dana Bea will fly out with the kids. I'll stay and help put her house together when the movers arrive. Sam will be somewhere in all of this mess; riding along, flying with us, or staying with Coach. He smiles and nods, "You got that right mama."

The boys secure an apartment, the girls are packed and ready for Dana to vacate. They are on their own, except for funds—we discuss money in private with Jessie.

"All of you Californians ready to head to the Lone Star Country?" No one moves, they just look back at me like I'm giving a speech at a seminar. I repeat," Hey, wake up out there, you guys ready for this?"

Dana Bea finally says, "Mom, you are making me feel tired." The girls smile and so do I.

"Sorry honey, but I can't put you on my back and walk you to Weatherford. It's okay honey, it's the unknown that causes anxiety."

Jessie puts meeting her biological father on the back burner. She has too much going on and besides, she says Archie will drive her there. Ray promises to give his oldest son pointers. Hansen has all of the paperwork and information from his trip north. Jessie is not as emotionally connected to her horrid past at the moment, and only has stars in her eyes for Archie.

We made it. Dana Bea finally she sees her new home and loves it. Yes, she is tired so I step up to help as much as I can without stepping on toes. When baby Abby naps, so does her mommy. Slowly she begins to come alive and choose paint colors, cook and play with Charlie, who is now a nice young boy and not an energy machine running helter skelter around in circles.

We move into our remodel and it is splendid. My favorite thing, besides the amazing cooks, is the veranda. I love to sit and listen to the Meadowlarks, even though I rarely see them. The sweet song lulls me into a restful space to daydream and be thankful.

One warm day, as we adjust to being Texans, the phone rings. Jessie and Archie tell us they have decided it's time to marry.

She excitedly tells us, "He asked me on the beach in the evening." She describes how he dropped to one knee and asked her and told her she is the only girl for him. They set the date for June 21, the solstice, it's on a Saturday. They schedule their wedding to be at the ranch, under the old oak tree. Here we go again, Sam listens and nods in agreement.

CHAPTER SIXTEEN

"Time for another party darlin'," he relays. Sam and I feel our age and are beginning to slow down a bit, but I think we can muster up one more wedding, and dance one more time, and eat an amazing Mexican feast just one more time. Dana Bea is thrilled and asks me to repeat the date. No problem, school will be out for the summer and Coach could use a good party.

Our family gathers together to discuss the plans. Ray and Peg and the rest of the *gang of ranch hands,* I am of course referring to the girls plus Ray and Peg's handsome sons.

I ask Jessie a few questions, "What about school, what about getting your degree, and what about your roommate Lea, will she be here also?"

"Yes, Lea is my maid of honor and her parents are coming, her big brother and her little sister."

"What about college Jessica?" I repeat.

"Yes, Grandma, we'll be in California until we both graduate and then we'll move to Texas."

I excuse myself, tell everyone I will be right back then head to the kitchen and mix myself a well needed tall cool Mint Julep. Jessie follows me towards the veranda, I look back to make sure she follows. "You are carrying a heavy load Jessie, and you are under a lot of pressure. Planning your wedding is one thing, college another, and all the while, on the back burner is your decision to meet your biological father and step inside a maximum security state prison. Confronting a stranger, is a lot of pressure for a young woman, for anyone actually. Are you ready?"

A FATHER'S CONFESSION

Jessie shrugs and confides, "I guess, I am more than frightened Grandma. I tremble at the thought of setting foot on the grounds, even the parking lot scares me. I will go when I am ready"

She leaves a message for Grandpa Sam to phone her, to make sure everything is in order. Sam calls back to make sure they remember to make an appointment. He gives her the number. Visiting is Saturday and Sundays only. He reminds her to dress with modesty. No skirts above the knee, nothing tight fitting to disclose a shapely figure, or you will be sent to the parking lot. Sam suggest she wear slacks, not too tight, and a long sleeve cotton blouse.

"Be prepared darlin' you and Archie will have to go through a medal detector. Everyone does. He reminds her, you will only have ten minutes to talk. Your name as an accepted visitor along with Archie's is in their system."

Jessica tells Grandpa Sam, "It's time Grandpa, I need to get this out of my head and put it behind me before my wedding day. Grandpa, I need to confront him and hopefully get some closure on the beatings he inflicted upon me. I think I can relax easier once this is behind me."

Sam hangs up the phone and tells me, "Your little girl is growing up. Let's go sit outside under the shade tree, eh Nettie gal?"

Grandpa Sam boasts, "I marvel at Jessie's spirit and determination." I am quiet, deep in thought.

They fly to the Medford, Oregon airport with all the needed paperwork and ID. Sam gives them another stern warning about visitation, and cautions them to be careful and be prepared. First and foremost, don't be conned by a con-man.

CHAPTER SIXTEEN

"Don't reveal any towns, colleges or personal information and particularly, your last names." Sam reminds them.

Jessica marvels at the beautiful scenic drive, the cliffs and jagged rock formations and the never ending ocean making powerful crashes when the waves hit the rocks. This is a surprise. She takes in the dramatic show of white foam and powerful waves, smashing against the cliffs, then reaching to the sky and then slowly receding back to make more waves. "This part of the ocean is more violent than where I grew up," Jessie observes.

When they see a view of a beach, they notice the sandy beaches are covered with thousands of pieces of drift wood, cast from the violent ocean. It's a long drive, but they couldn't stop looking and waiting for the next wave. This scene makes it difficult to believe there is a prison in the area.

If it is possible for a prison to be in a great location, this is a prime example. The building is large but understated. She phones to tell us there are many small windows and a looming gray stucco building overlooking the bay. The shape seems to be set out like a star, or octopus. Archie said he is getting the creeps just driving so near. It is close to a fishing town that appears to get swallowed up in the fog more days than you'd want to live through. Jessie shivers thinking about the cool weather, gray skies, and the huge gray building that looms up out of nowhere. This vision gives them goose bumps.

They find a hotel for the night, they also discover a café overlooking the ocean. Jessie orders clam chowder in a bread bowl, and a small shrimp salad with sour dough bread. Archie orders halibut with a lemon butter sauce, vegetables and twice baked potato with melted cheese.

They enjoy the view, and search for fishing boats far out to sea. But these two are so full they can barely move with comfort in order to explore the area. Jessie later tells me, "It was almost like a honeymoon." I gulp at the thought.

The next morning, they drive in the direction of the prison. It is breathtakingly beautiful and verboten all mixed together. Nerves take over and even Archie has the jitters.

When they arrive, they sit in the car and hold hands. "Oh Archie, I am so scared. I can't do this."

He confesses he knows how she feels; angry, frightened, but also vulnerable and weak. He squeezes her hands together, they hug each other in the car; and still they procrastinate.

He takes a deep breath and says, "Okay Jessie, let's do this." They get out and walk in silence toward uncharted territory. They sign in, show their drivers licenses, and all their identity with a photo. They walk to the next window and announce they are here to visit with, Jessie's voice quivers, but she manages to choke out, "Richard Clute."

They have been prepared by former Ranger Sam, and so far everything seems to be running as smooth as silk. They wait longer than expected, twenty-five minutes, which doesn't help their nerves. The waiting room is full, twenty-two women not counting Jessie and Archie. Finally, the wide thick door makes a noise as if it is bolted, then unlocks and her name is called, she stands and walks towards the door with Archie next to her. They go through a metal detector and she puts her purse through the x-ray machine. Archie empties

CHAPTER SIXTEEN

his pockets. They gather their belongings and together walk down a long wide intimidating hallway. They are told to sit at number C4. She sits with her card, Archie next to her.

She shakes inside, and wants to bolt while Archie takes it all in, pointing out how much there is to absorb. "Jessie look around it's like a scene from the movies."

The guard walks behind a prisoner who has leg irons with a long chain around his waist and wrists. He shuffles in and looks to be about sixty years old, but is much younger. He has thinning hair that used to be blonde and piercing blue eyes. He has no idea who sits on the other side of the glass. He assumes it's a fan, a sympathizer, or someone he met on an online prison dating site. Rich sits as instructed, both wrists cuffed. He picks up the phone, and points for her to do the same. She obeys.

He is friendly, and somewhat coy. He says, "Well hello there, and what may I do you for?" Jessie swallows hard and tells this unsuspecting egomaniac convict the shocking news.

"My name is Holly, I am your daughter, the toddler who went missing." Unable to speak he falls back in his chair, presses the back side of the phone to his mouth, and tears fill his eyes.

He looks at her features, leans forward and looks straight into her eyes as if she is not real, perhaps a figment on his imagination. His lips quiver as he says, "I am so sorry Holly, so very sorry."

She is also crying but digs deep to find the strength to ask her father, "Why did you beat me so hard, so often, why, what did I do to make you so mad?"

A FATHER'S CONFESSION

He wipes his eyes with his calloused hands and answers, "I don't know, I just, well, when I drink, and do lines I get real angry. I guess I took it out on you because you were there, my only outlet."

He adds, "Holly, that is the reason I did it."

She responds in an inquiring innocent way, "Did what, beat me?"

"Holly, when I got sober I knew I would kill you if I didn't do something, you know, make a move, so one night, I picked you up, and carried you up the hill and hid you under that lady's tree, that tree next to her porch." Jessica listens, stunned.

"I tossed a limb and hit the side of her house, I waited across the street, waiting for her to come outside to look around."

Jessie is shocked and asks, "You put me there?"

Rich nods, "Yes, I did, I put you under the tree and told you to stay put and not move a muscle, then I ran off and waited. I walked past her house and called out for you, acting angrier than I was, so she'd believe you were lost." He goes on, "I stomped off into the night, screaming for you. Then went down the street and hid behind some bushes, I crouched down and didn't smoke because I thought she might see my cigarette. I watched from down the street. I saw her walk down the steps and walk towards the tree. I watched her pick you up and I saw you crawl inside her night robe. She walked you back up the steps and into her house. I knew she would keep you."

Jessica is dumbfounded with Rich's unexpected confession, she sits there, confused and hurt. Rich goes on to tell her, "I knew when she and I guess ... her friend   ... or daughter, walked past our house,

CHAPTER SIXTEEN

they were checking us out. They even took pictures, then put on a big fake scene about my car. I knew I had to make a change or you would die and I was afraid they might turn me in."

Jessica keeps at him, "Where is my mother?"

His red eyes looked down, this is a bad sign. Rich quietly says, "Robin clocked out about five years ago, overdosed on smack."

Jessica asks, "What is that word?

He asks, "You mean smack?" She nods. "Heroin, too much, she died instantly."

"When I went missing did she cry for me?"

"Yes baby, she did, but she cried for herself too."

"We were a mess Holly, we just got totally messed up. Girl, I'm still messed up," he confesses.

"It looks like that lady took good care of you Holly. You look real pretty; you look like my sister Rose."

"You have a sister Rose, where is she?"

"Rosie lives in Yreka. It's a real pretty town."

Jessie asks him for Rose's phone number and he rattles it off. Archie is great with numbers and memorizes it very quickly. Jessie takes a deep breath, then gets the courage to ask him a very important question.

A FATHER'S CONFESSION

"Rich, sorry, I mean dad, do you remember my birth date?"

He smiles, and is somewhat cocky to be the only one with this answer, he leans forward and looks right into her face and says, "October 21, 1982. You came into the world at 6:29 A.M. Damn, Robin had a real hard time too, but then all at once, there you were, so tiny. She named you Holly Rose." Jessie gulps, since she has not revealed her middle name. She is pleased but needs to move on with more questions.

Rich, "What did you do to be put in here? This is a very serious high security prison."

He corrects her and informs her, "This is beyond high security. This is called a supermax prison. Housed here are the worst of the worst." Rich tells her his story, "Got drunk, got mad at some dude, damn, he just kept at me and I beat him to death, he started the fight, I finished it. It was my third offense, which means three strikes, have you ever heard of that Holly?"

She swallows hard, "I have not."

Rich goes on to explain, "When you get three strikes, like in baseball, you know, you get caught three times, well the third time the law throws away the key. Holly, I know I have a loose wire. I know I am a danger to society. I know this is where I need to be, it's okay, don't worry about me. Just please forgive me."

"The woman who took me in took photos, and cleaned me up." She tells him. "I was shown photos of open wounds, bruising, and scars on my backside and face. I came to fear you and hate you. I still have scars on my back and legs, and they will be with me for the rest of my life."

CHAPTER SIXTEEN

Jessie gains power and says, "The lady who rescued me saved my life and gave me an education and lots and lots of love. She told me that the night she found me, she tended to my wounds, and was gentle with me. She loves me."

Rich sits very still and listens while tears stream down his face. He looks at her through the glass and speaks into the phone, "Then I did the right thing, for once in my stupid dirty life I did the right thing, damn straight, and I got away with it, and I didn't fuck anything up." He seems proud of his plan and the outcome and goes on, "Holly, I'm sorry I gave you so much pain. I am very sorry baby girl."

Jessie stops, decides to move on and get off this very touchy subject, she looks up and puts her hand on Archie's that rests on her shoulders for support, and introduces him. "*Dad,* this is Archie, we're getting married next month. We met in Texas and we both attend a University in California."

Rich replies, "Very proud to meet your son, good to know an educated man." He looks back at Jessica and blurts out, "I have a kid in college, that's so very damn cool Kiddo, yeah Holly!" This seemingly innocent response shocks Jessie because her real name keeps rolling off his tongue with such ease, *her real name,* Holly flows and she feels her healing process begin.

Rich has tattoos on his wrists, forearms and neck, and he has bad teeth, but she detects he was, at one time a handsome man. He has great bone structure, but now he is a broken man whose life has come full circle. During the entire visit Rich asks for nothing. He is sorry, apologetic and proud; all rolled into one.

A FATHER'S CONFESSION

Archie whispers, "Honey, you only have two minutes left."

Holly rushes into her speech, "Well Richard, ah, I mean *dad*, it's been nice meeting you, and I must to tell you something before we leave, I really need to tell you this in case we never meet again. I forgive you. With all my heart, I forgive you, sleep well daddy, Sleep well." She presses on, "Thank you for doing what you did, it was truly a selfless act, to place me where you knew she'd find me. I will always feel compassion for you. Thank you."

Archie steps forward, nods and says, "Sir," then steps back.

Rich hangs the phone back on the cradle then reaches out and puts his trembling hand on the glass, He looks at Jessie and ignores the tears as they run along the deep grooves of his weather lined face. Without thought she automatically mimics his gesture, reaches towards the glass and places her delicate hand against the glass so they can touch, without touching.

A red light blinks, and the phone goes dead.

CHAPTER SIXTEEN

They ride south looking for the turn off. This drive is much different than heading north. It is scenic, breathtaking really, but Jessie is quiet, and in a dark place.

She puts her hand on Archie's and says, "I thought this visit would bring closure for me, but it dredged up some suppressed feelings I didn't know I had. I guess I need something more, or maybe less."

Archie pulls over at one of the rest areas, they are surrounded by giant redwoods. They sit in the car and look at the bluffs. They don't speak, they sit and look at the ocean and the crashing waves. They watch with fatigue and silence.

She finally turns to him and confesses, "I'm fine, really, I just need to process this visit."

Archie isn't sure how far to go with his impression or opinions so he squeezes her small hand and tells her to take all the time she needs, a lifetime if necessary.

Off they go, south down the coastline, which seems like another world away. He turns east, and they follow a shady road lined with Redwoods and ferns, to eventually lead them toward Grants Pass. He spots a diner and they decide this might be what they need, food. This café, nestles in under the pines seems inviting and safe. Once inside the café named Audrey's, they notice raw rustic plank walls, and decorations of handmade wreaths and local art, a redhead hands them menus. They read the paper menu, the food looks normal, you know, basic. They order and wait. Jessie looks very tired and aged. Archie is in a quiet space too. The plates arrive and it is enough food for two truck drivers. Authentic country style lunch mixed with breakfast style fried onions, eggs and potatoes, biscuits and gravy with bits of

A FATHER'S CONFESSION

bacon, a square of cornbread and a few pieces of watermelon. In their shocked state they begin to stuff themselves They have to put their hands over their mouths to laugh.

"Oh my goodness Archie, this meal is insane," Jessie chokes out. He nods yes with his head, his mouth full of food. Today is the first time he hears her burp. She giggles and says, "Oh, sorry." They pay their tab and jump into the car.

"Life is going to be okay for us, this is closure for you Jessie, you are so brave to go there and confront him. I am so proud of you honey."

She gives a slight smile and coos, "Thank you Archie."

They breeze past Grants Pass and in no time, they arrive at the Medford airport.

Back home she has the task of telling me about the visit. But Jessica is too worn out, too stripped of emotions to talk. She has Archie tell Sam that she needs some space and time to recap her encounter with Rich. Sam is happy he stayed behind, "These kids needed to experience this journey together."

Two weeks later Jessica feels strong enough. She phones late one morning and suggests to me to please sit down. Jessica describes a cold and foggy place. I listen and think to myself, "Good, I hope he is cold and prays for the sun to come out, and I hope it never does."

Sam sees my face and softly says, "Settle down Buffalo Bill."

Then she reconstructs the Pelican Bay supermax prison, the visit and the astonishing truth of the night I found her under the tree.

CHAPTER SIXTEEN

I exclaim, "How could he have known this, it must true." I think out loud, "Why did the men follow us and investigate us for so many years?"

"Grandma, I think they thought we did an exchange, not a kidnapping. I'm sure they suspected him from the beginning since he never reported me missing." I am dumbfounded, and feel played.

"He should have simply brought you to my home, knocked on my door like a normal person. Not put you under a tree in the snow. He has no integrity or a lick of sense," I fume.

"Oh Grandma, "He did what he knew to do, which was something sneaky and something honorable rolled into one. He knew he'd kill me if he wasn't stopped," she offers in his defense.

"Yes, okay dear, I'm sorry. I regret saying negative things about your dad. I will try to see the good." I dig deep for this promise.

I struggle to find a shred of honor in Rich Clute. His decision of abandonment, to distance himself from his young daughter saves her life. His generous gift is sprinkled with stupidly. Imagine if I had not come outside to find her. What if a bear came down from the foothills, or she toddles off into the woods? Then it hits me; Rich and Robin were questioned at length by the police regarding the whereabouts of their missing daughter. I am sure Robin was not in on his notion to hide her in the snow, or she would have stopped him. I hope and only assume this. The fact remains, they never told the police their daughter Holly, was with me.

I accept this notion and realize that Rich did save his daughter's life by pretending to be searching and angry that cold night. Now I need

A FATHER'S CONFESSION

time to process the past years, and his clever plan. She and Sam sit outside and rehash the revelations of Jessica being found under Nettie's Dogwood.

I stew on this for a day or two and it keeps coming back to this; Rich has many dark qualities, but he is not a snitch. A miniscule of compassion fills my heart, as I unfold his web of inappropriate choices.

Sam stands up and says to her, "Good job my Jessie girl, you are a very brave soul." Sam changes the subject and says, "Now let's put this on the shelf and plan a wedding."

CHAPTER SEVENTEEN

Wedding Bells

JESSIE, ARCHIE AND LEA FLY INTO DALLAS one week before the big day. The energy of these kids is contagious. They know what they want and need, and how to go about it. Archie is in command of Cody, who is wrapped around Lea. Archie orders his brother to step away and get to work. Lots of teasing and laughter. The kids arrange for Charlie to come up for a few days. Grandpa Sam drives over to Weatherford to pick him up. Charlie is a helpful kid, a surprising change since our wedding day.

Jessie is very private about her plans and to some degree this upsets her Grandma. Dana Bea cautions me, "Be gentle and back away. You have done your work raising a beautiful girl, a college girl, pat yourself on the back and let her do this her way."

CHAPTER SEVENTEEN

The music begins and out steps little Abigale with a little pink dress, tossing light pink and dark pink rose pedals. Out comes Charlie carrying a pillow with two rings. There stands Cody in a gray suit sporting a cowboy hat, he stands next to his brother Archie who wears a matching suit, a thin satin silver tie, he also wears Sam's grandfather's silver spurs. So far so good. Seems this will be a flawless production.

A woman sings the wedding march with a young girl playing the violin in the background. Jessica steps out of the barn wearing a floor length white silk gown with lace sleeves. She is lovely, and looks like an angel. She holds a large bouquet of pink roses. I look at her from head to toe when, at this instant I realize she's wearing my sister's wedding dress. Abigale is with us. I can hardly look at Jessica as she proudly stands next to Archie.

This is the surprise she has been keeping locked up so tight. It is a struggle, but I keep my composure in check, put my hand to my mouth and with my other hand I squeeze Sam's. He knew all along, he bends down and kisses my cheek. Now we have the girls crying, Dana Bea and Jessie have red eyes and Lea is tearing up too; outcome the hankies.

Meaningful vows, music and kissing. I am kind of a mess and not really paying as close attention as I should. All I see is Abigale, standing in the same dress.

The crowd erupts into a roar of clapping and whoops and everyone smiles. I sit quietly, feeling sad and in shock, and feel I'm losing my grip.

The spread of food is fit for a king and queen, we eat, drink, toast the newlyweds, and chat while the band sets up. It's a different band, a country band that also plays rock and roll.

WEDDING BELLS

I retreat to the veranda and absorb this day and events. I just can't get focused, unable to find my happy spot. I guess too much has happened lately. I am still in shock that her biological father actually gave her to me. I am thankful to him, but it is very difficult to fear and hate someone, then praise them. I know I can do it, but today is too soon.

What was meant as a pleasant surprise, an honor, takes me back to a dark time, and I can't seem to shake it off.

Here comes Sam up the staircase. He bends down and whispers in my ear, "Come on Grandma, you can do it, Jessica needs you to be with her, as you always have been."

He hugs me a long while and rocks me back and forth as he always has. Hand in hand we walk down the staircase back to the reception. I hold little Abby and help guide food into her mouth, with a towel tucked under her chin, just like I used to put on Jessica. Her pretty pink dress will stay that way, pink.

Abby reaches up with her tiny hand and touches my necklace, and says, "Mine."

I say, "No it's Grandma's."

She repeats, "Mine."

I am straight forward and say, "Maybe one day it will be yours, but tonight is belongs to Grandma." The words are confusing to her but she lets it go. Charlie is off with his daddy and everyone enjoys the festivities.

I look towards my daughter, and she mouths, "You okay?"

CHAPTER SEVENTEEN

I nod and smile back at her beautiful face. It is not easy to jump into this wild party, but I do find peace holding this beautiful little girl, who is hell bent on taking my necklace. Abby did such a good job today as the flower girl, yes indeed. Abby slides off my lap and down my leg. I wipe dry cereal off my skirt and I tell her, "Find Grandpa," then point the way. She trots off towards him.

Jessie whoops and is dancing with Lea, then walks towards Archie. The rock and rollers are in high gear and nothing will stop them. When the music is over I feel arms around my neck, I look backwards to see Jessie hugging me.

"I love you Grandma. I'm so happy," she curls her head around to the side of my face and goes on, "I know I'm young, but this is my destiny and I am going to embrace this day."

I pat her hands and tell her she is lovely in her Aunt Abigale's dress. "She would be so pleased to witness this union."

Jessie hugs me and says, "She is with us." We tip our heads together touching foreheads.

"I love my life and family." She yells as she runs off.

Jessica darts off into the night, back to the dance floor. Lea's parents are dancing. Archie, Jessie, Cody and Lea, and the boys' parents. Charlie dances alone. Everyone is having the time of their life.

Dana Bea runs towards me and asks if I can watch Abby while she rounds up Coach for a slow dance. There she goes, running off into the night in her tight plum colored dress, sexy and classy. Abby runs towards me, I squat down and reach out with waiting arms. Charlie runs off the dance floor and climbs up onto a bale of hay and jumps off. I watch Coach and my lovely daughter sway back and forth to a song called, *The Most Beautiful Girl in the World*. Then Abby runs back to her Grandpa and begins to climb up on his leg, he looks back at me, I wink and I wave back. I look around and find Jessica and Archie slow dancing and talking real close, one of the former Rangers yells, "Hey, get a room," every one claps and whoops. Lea and Cody are just as close, Sam walks off to the side talking to some good ol' boys, yes, former Rangers, and sends Abby running back to me.

The next morning the family gathers in the main part of the house to eat and visit. Everyone in the room notices the dust explosion barreling down the road, it's Archie and Jessie. They want to be with family and have breakfast before flying off to Cancun this evening. What a relaxed fun day with country foods and lots of coffee and chatter.

Breakfast eaters slowly push away from the table. Most of us meet in the living room to lay around and moan. Coach wants to talk to Sam and Ray about his football team. Dana is dressing the kids and finally comes downstairs to relax and curl up in a fluffy chair. Carmelita takes the kids with her back to the kitchen. From the kitchen we hear much laughter and noise as the sisters clean up. Ramona stays outside talking to Hector.

I tell Sam, "I think we might have another wedding coming up."

Cody comes in and stands there under the wide arch. He waits a minute then announces he has something to say. Everyone stops what they are doing and looks at Cody; who is normally off with a gang of boys, and is usually the quietest of Ray's two boys.

CHAPTER SEVENTEEN

Cody clears his throat, waits, then announces that he has enlisted in the Army. I thought his dad was going to fall out of his chair. An uncomfortable moment of silence fills the room.

"Yep, I enlisted, then one day when I'm out, I'll have benefits and get my own place and start a family." He proudly announces.

I stay quiet, Archie jumps up and hugs his brother, whispers something in his ear. Lea, in a louder voice than expected says, "What? Cody, are you sure?"

Sam shakes his hand and his dad and mom stand with him and explain that they will talk at home. His mom is trying to hold back a whole bunch of tears and emotions. His dad is stoic.

Archie and Jessica politely excuse themselves and say it's time to head to the airport, you know how it is these days with a two hour waiting period to board and all. Dana Bea watches people interact and stays quiet. I wait my turn to give Cody a nice big hug. Coach steps up and slaps him on the back then pulls him in for a hug and a handshake.

I'm not sure how I feel about this. I think it's best to stay neutral and let his family have their own discussion.

It is 2004 the war in Afghanistan rages. I thought they were going to be in and out of there but this war is still a dangerous hot spot with no end in sight. Capturing Saddam Hussein in Iraq where he is now in prison is a huge event. His trial will begin soon and we'll have to wait and see what happens. We are still looking for the weapons of mass destruction.

WEDDING BELLS

We seem so far removed from this suffering and hatred. Cody is a wonderful young man, I sure hate to see him join the fight. He is just not a fighter.

Cody's mother Peg is very upset, as is his dad. But Ray is also a stand-up guy who has always encouraged his sons to do the admirable thing. Cody says he's been talking to a recruiter for a while now. He never told a soul. I'm sure Lea feels betrayed with this secrecy that could change the course of his future, and hers too. But this is Cody's path, and everyone accepts his decision.

The brothers have a nice long talk outside, then hug and pat each other on the back. Cody kisses Jessie on the cheek. Lea stands next to him holding his hand, they walk off towards stacks of baled hay. They sit and talk. I can see she is very upset and he comforts her. They embrace and continue to talk.

I have to wonder why he would make this announcement the morning after his brother's wedding. His speech initially breaks up the room and chatter and upsets his parents. His brother and bride Jessica are surprised and upset, not to mention his girlfriend, who is beside herself. It just seemed like a bad idea. Maybe he felt this was the best time since everyone was together. Our family is as easy to bring together as herding cats. That must be the reason he chose the post wedding breakfast.

The ranch is quiet, everyone is in their own world, while Cody prepares for boot camp. He runs and exercises everyday so he won't be a target for the drill sergeant. He watched *Stripes* and laughs a lot and decides he is not going to be a Bill Murray solider.

CHAPTER SEVENTEEN

The honeymooners arrive back at the ranch and both are tan and in very giggly moods. They are greeted with hugs and joy.

The time is growing near, Sam visits Ray often. I stay with Dana Bea to help her with cooking and caring for the kids, while Coach works. Archie tells Jessie he is staying in Texas until his brother leaves. He jumps in and helps Cody with exercise and running long distances. They build obstacle courses for both of them to try out. It's a lot of fun for these nonstop brothers. Jessica says she'll stay too. The brothers workout and wait. I tend to the kids when needed and dote on my handsome husband, and we wait. Jessie shows me photos taken of Cancun this includes being on a fishing boat and snorkeling. She marvels at the extra-large marble tiles in the hotel's entry and the massive swimming pool at the hotel with water features. She is beaming and very happy. I watch her and realize, she is part of my problem. I thought I'd be raising her forever. Jessie went from a young playful girl doing cartwheels across the beach, to giggles at slumber parties and helping me decorate cookies, to a married woman. I am not prepared to let her go.

It was easier for Dana Bea, for she has been on her path since birth. Everything was as it should be and she is very self-supporting and self-reliant. She was also out of college and had a job. Jessica likes to stay with me to cook, and color, talk and cuddle up with me under thick blankets. This continued up until she was a senior in high school. Somethings take time, and letting this little bird go is not an easy transition.

CHAPTER EIGHTEEN

Saying Goodbye

THE DAY ARRIVES AND ONCE AGAIN we have a full house. Cody's going away party is twofold, proud and fearful. Oh how his mother cried. Cody is brave and very tender with her. He and his dad have a moment and then Lea has her turn. Yes, there is Lea who clings to him and promises to write every day. He keeps his cool. Then without any fanfare he is out the door with his parents and brother. They take Cody off to boot camp via the Dallas airport, leaving Lea behind.

Jessie stays back, out of respect for this family unit and I am thrilled to have her all to myself. Lea is here too, but not really here. She stays in her room at the ranch and cries most of the day. Jessie comes downstairs, we have many long afternoons to visit and talk about life, her real dad, and her marriage. I take advantage of this time and off we go into the kitchen for a week of cooking lessons.

We name this cooking class, "Beyond Cookies." Lea finally joins us and we make casseroles, a pot roast and all the trimmings, spaghetti with meatballs, lasagna, and fresh homemade soup. I know from these dishes

CHAPTER EIGHTEEN

she can go any direction in a kitchen. This Thanksgiving we will get into the lesson of how to trim the bird.

School is to begin soon, Jessica and Lea fly back to San Luis Obispo with Archie. It is bitter sweet for them, and very painful for Archie. He helps get the girls settled in, then he and Jessie move into her room. But no matter what they do, Cody is on everyone's mind.

The semester begins and the days move into fall, then winter. The kids fly home for the holidays and Jessica helps right along with the cooks. Lea stays back to be with her family. The kids spend time staying with Archie's parents. It is a quiet time, the kids love all the food and desserts, and we adults are thankful Cody is safe.

Winter blows in with wind and rain, and brings violent weather conditions. Crackling thunder and lightning are upon us. We curl up in warm blankets and watch movies and wait for it to pass.

The newlyweds return to the ranch for their school break. Spring peeks its head around the corner and with it arrives a flurry of flowers. Along our fence that guards our yard from tumbleweed and cattle, Texas Bluebonnets begin to pop up their heads. They add color and beauty to this barren land, and seem to be everywhere. Reminds me of all the Poppys in California.

Archie spends hours with Coach tossing baskets in the gym while Sam and Ray yell from the bleachers. Jessica and Dana Bea connect and she helps her with babysitting so she and Coach can enjoy alone time and a date night. Time seems to drag on, it's supposed to be spring, but the winds are still cold and whip around in circles. Tumbleweeds fly around the house like attacks dogs. The wind is brutal and makes us all crazy. My flowers suffer greatly.

SAYING GOODBYE

In late May, we fly out with Ray and Peg, to attend Archie, Jessica and Lea's graduations. Lea is graduating with a Bachelors of Arts, and Jessica with a Bachelor of Science.

The sun rises, it's an amazing day, we scrunch in with hundreds of families and wait. We see sun hats galore. The girls graduate earlier in the day, Archie in the afternoon.

When each girl walks across the stage it is Dana Bea's graduation all over again. I remember Jim and how difficult it was to be there without him. I hear them call Jessica's name and I want to stand on my chair and scream. The feeling of accomplishment and love mixed with determination engulfs me. Then Lea's group walks out and still, the same feelings. I can't help but remember these little girls running around on the sandy beach, coming together for sleepovers, packing their favorite blankets with their well-worn stuffed animals. There they are, tossing their caps high into the air.

When they call his name, Archie walks across the stage in his cap and gown; we friends and family stand and scream and clap. Well-meaning hugs suffocate Archie, then all the graduates toss their caps high up into the air.

We hit some pubs and toast the graduates, we feast on a large lunch of deep fried fish and chips. It is great to be back by the ocean. The mild weather and the familiar never ending breeze completes the day.

Sam and I sneak off for some alone time and realize we are hopeless homing pigeons. We drive back to our complex to recall where it all began. We run to the beach and look back. Our duplexes are smaller than I remember, and not as tidy. Instead of a cute table and chairs on the patio, I see three bikes wrapped with cables for security, buckets for

CHAPTER EIGHTEEN

playing in the sand, and towels draped over the rail. We walk out to the shoreline holding hands and look back again for a longer view.

He scoops me up into his arms and I yell, "Your ankle Sam, careful now honey."

He lets out a whoop and says, "Now don't get your dress wet darlin'."

"I yell over the sound of waves, "You wouldn't!"

He laughs and says, "Well I would have, but today, graduation day, nah."

He sets me safely down, then we run down the shore, our feet touching the incoming foam that creeps up from the tide. Then youth gets the best of him and he scoops me up and off we go into the ocean. I scream like a child and he laughs so hard I prepare to be dropped, right there on the beach. Sam is laughing hysterically, but somehow we make it to the water. Before I can say no way buster, I fly through the air then come up for breath. I recall how much fun it is, being tossed into the ocean. He jumps in after me, we stand in the ocean and kiss. I tell him I hope the rest of our family is as spontaneous, because we have so much fun.

He says, "Well, someone has to run the show, so let's you and I show them by example." Together we walk along on the warm sand, and don't stop until our cloths are dry.

Today it is one long day of eating and celebration. There is a knock at the door, Lea heads to the door, opens it and there stands Cody. He has a ten-day pass, and he knew his parents and family would be here for graduation. He requested California.

SAYING GOODBYE

Lea asks, "For how long?"

He says, "Ten days." Oh boy, you could have blown the roof off. Archie phones his parents at the hotel. Archie tells them they need to come over, it's an emergency. Since Cody had a car rental, his parents have no idea. Within ten minutes Ray and Peg arrive at Dana Bea's house, which is now the kid's rental. They rush to the front door, knock and wait, Cody opens the door. His parents scream like they'd just been doused with snowballs.

It is the perfect day—graduation and Cody home—at least he is back on American soil. I phone my daughter and tell her how thoughts of her fill my head, being at the same stadium and all. It was fun, wish you and your family were here too. She sighs, too much hassle to pack and travel with the kids. It is nice to stay home and relax with Coach. Besides, "I don't want to see the inside of my rental." We laugh a little.

When we return back to our ranch, Dana Bea stops by with the kids to visit and asks us about the graduation. She asks about Cody showing up, so I had to recap this great moment. She looks and notices my clothes outside on the line, blowing in the breeze.

"Mother, what is that on your clothes line? It that your new dress?"

I answer, "Yes dear, it shrunk."

"Mother you and Sam did not—yes you did—oh my goodness you two, you are too old, stop letting him toss you into the ocean, you are not a beach ball!" She exclaims.

CHAPTER NINETEEN

Growing Pains

Archie lands a job as the Deputy Agriculture Commissioner in Parker County. The County gives him three weeks to find a house and get settled. The Parker County Seat happens to be Weatherford. I can't believe it! The kids fly to Dallas and drive straight on to Weatherford, to meet with the realtor. They begin the exhausting chore of searching for a home. Then we have a family meeting and decide they should rent first, and get the lay of the land, and not rush into buying and paying too much. Dana Bea and Coach did their purchase straight off, but they knew themselves better and knew their likes and dislikes. They have also both been previous home owners. Jessica and Archie are young and have never lived in a house together, except to rent Dana Bea's place with roommate Lea.

They find a duplex across from a park, within walking distance to downtown where Archie's office is located, and only a few miles from Dana Bea and Coach's place.

Dana Bea calls a realtor in San Luis Obispo to put her house on the market. Then Dana Bea informs Lea, "Sorry, no more renting, we are selling."

CHAPTER NINETEEN

Dana Bea hires a painter to do the inside and out, and a cleaning service to clean. She hires a gardener to get the yard in selling shape. Lea is perplexed but decides to rent a room in an apartment. She is ready for a small space.

Cody is not going to win any ribbons for letter writing. He enjoys receiving mail, but rarely answers. Of course he is in the Middle East in the heat of a war; we get that. Lea is patient and very scared, and her feelings have become a daily stress factor. He has a ten-day rest and recreation scheduled and asks Lea to meet him. The Army will pay for her flight and their stay. She takes the time off from her part time job, and her parents send her off with hugs.

They lay on the beach, snorkel and take long walks. Cody is not the same guy she'd met so long ago. He seems solemn, brooding inside. She has no idea how to reach him and comfort him. They hug, stay in their room, eat great foods, but something is wrong, something she can't fix. He won't engage in conversation. What he really wants and needs is quiet time, alone time. Lea takes her cue and lets him be. She has a massage and a milk bath. She shops for sarongs and other trinkets. She eats alone and waits for Cody to show up. The tenth day is coming up and he finally comes back to her. They lay on the beach and relax, snuggle and enjoy sex. He seems a little bit better, but he is frightened, and angry inside.

Lea is 23 years old, finishing up her last year of student teaching. Cody never asks her any questions concerning her life. She totally understands his inner conflict, and continues to stay quiet and out of his way.

Time creeps by, and as before, no letters from Cody.

She ponders the possibilities and decides she needs to be near her best friend Jessica and closer to Cody. She also admits to herself, she doesn't want to teach.

Her credentials help her in her job search. She sends out resumes all over the state and accepts a job offer on the Texas Gulf Coast.

Her boss is Josh Rivera. He has thick black hair and no accent. She asks him if he is Mexican and he smiles and says, "No, my mother married Juan Rivera when I was a small boy, and I took his last name." Josh teaches her the company's job skills and makes sure she is working well with the others and understands her job description.

One day, a Friday, he asks her if she would like to catch dinner after work. It is a big mistake to date a coworker, much less your boss. She declines, but Josh piques her interest. She has not heard from Cody and Jessie tells her, "Archie waits for a letter or word, but we hear nothing, same for his parents."

Josh is slightly graying on the sides of his dark hair. "Premature graying," he calls it. She is smitten but keeps her feelings hidden.

One night while out at a nightclub with friends from her apartment complex in walks Josh. Oh no! She picks up her phone and calls Jessica. She can't tell her what is really going on because she'll tell Archie. Lea just says hello to Jessie and tells her she wishes she was here, and she misses her so much. Her plea for support goes haywire.

Josh sees her and walks over, "May I buy you a drink?" Well, she stammers, "Isn't that against company rules?"

CHAPTER NINETEEN

He smiles and asks, "What would you like?"

She responds with, "White wine please." They end up with a table by the sea and order shrimp cocktails and continue to sip their drinks. She tells him about Cody, California, Cal Poly, Jessica, her family, brother and sister and about San Luis Obispo.

He tells her about his life in the gulf, his mother, his step dad and his college days. They talk well into the night. Last call, it's 1:45 A.M. they have so much more to tell each other.

Lea has never met a man who is so interesting, straight forward and interested in her. He is tall, and sexy and older. She asks him how old he is and he says, "Thirty-six." He knows her age, her address, her college classes; he has read her resume.

They say goodbye and he asks her to meet him again. This company romance goes on through most of the summer and into the fall. He invites her to his apartment and he is invited to hers. He invites her to his mother's house for the holidays. She accepts, but not until she confides to her mother, and tells her there is no time to be in two states at the same time. Her mother understands, but is disappointed and says they will miss her and repeats. "No worries." Her mother confides, "I won't mention any of this to Jessica."

The following holiday she asks him to join her in California. He accepts. Their relationship takes off at record speed and she doesn't care if they are caught in a company relationship or not. He is the one.

She writes Cody and gently explains she has been thinking and it seems logical they should part ways. Lea goes on to say her life has taken a turn, she hopes the best for him and a safe return home. He finally replies and is hurt but understands. He tells her he isn't ready for a relationship anyway. It ends peacefully.

Christmas is wonderful, Lea loves the beaches and food and palm trees and the feel this beachy town has to offer. His family is wealthy and thrilled their son has met someone educated and from California. On New Year's Eve they bring in the celebration, then Josh drops to one knee and asks Lea to be his wife.

He is older, well, thirteen years older, "Is that a lot?" she wonders. Yes, I guess it is in some circles, but she doesn't care, she'd marry him if he was twice her age.

They take a long weekend trip to see Jessica and Archie. She confides to Jessie about this new older man in her life, and Jessica totally understands. She tells Lea she has always thought Cody was distant. He is a great guy, nice, polite, cute, blonde and sexy, but he just never seems like he is going to commit. Lea and Jessie have old fashioned girl talk. She tells her, "Josh is very tall and dark and handsome, then giggles. "Don't be surprised when you see gray hair on the sides, and I think he has even more gray since we met." Both girls howl at this concept.

They finally arrive in Weatherford, and find Jessie's duplex. Archie is on his way home from work. All is well and they look forward to a great long weekend. The girls talk about her job, living alone in an apartment, how she and Josh met and all that girly chatter.

Jessie whispers to Lea in the bathroom, "I missed my period."

CHAPTER NINETEEN

Lea screams "What! Jessie, what the heck—do you really think?"

"Ugh" she whispers. "Well I don't know, maybe. I'm not going to mention this to Archie until I take a test."

More great meals, then they toss a volley ball in Jessie's back yard for a while, relax and enjoy being with each other again. These childhood friends also get to know each other on a more adult level. Archie and Josh seem to get along, understand each other's jobs and both were born and raised in Texas.

On their way out of town Lea phones and asks me if they can stop by the ranch. She tells me about breaking up with Cody. I understand and tell her, "You did the right thing, you must be compatible for the long haul, and if you are not feeling loved, that is a red flag Lea."

Josh pulls up to the ranch and tells Lea this all seems very familiar. They park and walk to the back door, facing the barn, Sam yells, "Come on in."

There, face to face Sam stares at Josh.

Lea never mentioned how much she loves Josh's crooked smile, and his quick wit.

Sam looks at him and says, "Josh?"

"Is that you, come on in boy."

Josh is mute, dumbfounded, "Ah, Sam?"

"Please come in, we have a lot of catching up to do." Sam holds the screen door wide open, he opens his arms and gives Josh a long overdue hug with some back slaps.
Lea stands in silence trying to grasp the situation and what just transpired between her fiancée and Sam.

Lea speaks in all innocence, "Josh, I'd like to introduce you to Jessica's Grandpa Sam."

The two men shake, and enjoy the game. Then Josh turns to Lea and says, "Lea, I'd like to introduce you to my father, Sam."

The blood leaves Lea's face, she leans into Josh and whispers, "Your father?" She proceeds to stick her foot deeper into her mouth. "Oh yes right, I see you both have gray hair—oh yes, he has a crooked smile too."

I walk downstairs joyfully talking as I enter the room, "Sorry, I was finishing up." I hug Lea then hug Josh and introduce myself. "My goodness, you are a tall one." I then look at Sam, and quickly back to Josh and ask, "May I ask your last name?"

"Rivera."

I turn to Sam who looks like a dear in headlights.

I instantly know. Sam excuses himself and so does Josh, they walk into the living room, then out the back door. The silence is deathly. I sit down with Lea and hold her hand. "Now, isn't this a nice visit." I tell her how nice she looks and what a beautiful woman she has turned out to be.

CHAPTER NINETEEN

Lea says, "Nettie, what just happened, is this going to be a problem?"

I get up and bring in some bread and hot tea. No comment, just a polite smile.

"Now Lea, everything happens for a reason, and there is a much bigger plan, much larger than just you and I. Lea is wide eyed and listens. Let's go for a walk, would you like to gather eggs with me?"

Lea says, "Sure Nettie."

The men talk for two hours. Lunch is served, Sam decides to say a prayer over lunch. I look at him then towards Josh and bow my head.

"Dear Lord, thank you for returning my son to me. Thank you for your guidance and forgiveness. In our Heavenly Father's name, Amen."

"Damn, let's eat." They dive into a fabulous Mexican lunch, but the chatter does not flow.

I am speechless, Lea is dumbfounded, and Sam takes it in.

Jessie phones Lea the following Monday to confirm, yes, she is pregnant. Lea is quiet and tries to hold her secret tight to her chest.

She squeaks out, "Wow Jessie, I am so happy for you. You are only 22, but you are mature for your age, I know you'll be a great mom."

"No Lea, I'm 23 now, I didn't get a birthday card from you this year either!"

Lea apologizes and says "Well, with work and a new relationship, you know how it is." Their conversation is strained and they both know it. They chat, but it goes nowhere.
Lea phones Jessie back and asks her if she will be able to fly to California and be her maid of honor.

"When is your wedding"? Lea tells her, "July 1, you'll be in your sixth month."

Jessica laughs and asks Lea if she is a gynecologist. They share one of their silly moments.

"Yes, if all goes smoothly I will be there for you Lea, but in a dress with a high waist line, and in all my pregnant glory." Jessica sweetly responds.

Lea confides to Jessie about something she has kept from her and tells her it doesn't feel good. I want to tell you something and we hope this information can stay mum, we don't want it to get around." Jessie is startled, "Are you pregnant?"

She laughs, "Ha-ha, no silly. Ah, are you sitting down Jessie?"

Lea goes on, "Well, ah, well you met Josh and you know he is a lot older than me right, and well, then he met Sam and, well, gosh, as it turns out, Josh has been estranged from his dad since he was a little boy, and well Jessie …"

"Yeah, so, go on."

"He met Sam and Sam just happens to be Josh's dad."

CHAPTER NINETEEN

Loud scream, "What! What are you saying, oh, you said it, what the heck Lea!"

"Sam was the only one who was cool. So that's the secret, crazy huh!"

"Wow Lea, get out! You mean Sam is my grandpa and your father-in-law? Sweet, we will be related after all." The girls talk back and forth, once again best friends with easy high school chatter.

"Can I tell Archie?"

"Well, under the circumstances I'd say, please no. This news may be very difficult for Cody to absorb."

"Oh my God Lea, after I understand the huge impact of this connection, I'll call you back, love you Lea." Jessie calls Dana Bea first.

The wedding is in two weeks. Jessica is showing her baby bump and looks like she is hiding a small basketball under her shirt. I smother her with meals that I carefully transport to Weatherford. I also help her with shopping and general cleaning. I fuss over Jessica and visit with Dana and the kids.

We Texan guests flying out for the wedding are Jessie, Archie, Dana, Coach, Charlie, Abby, Sam and me—all on the same flight. Josh's mother Michelle and his step-dad Juan made their flight own plans. The next morning, July 1, we drive to the outskirts of town towards the wine country. The small chapel is located in Avila Beach and next door is a wine tasting room and banquet room. Jessie will wear a short dress deep blue, the color of the ocean, with a high waist and a shiny black belt right under her bosom. The dress is tight and cups her belly. I comment, "It's the new thing now, to show off your unborn baby. It looks great on you Jessie, with the high cut of this dress, it exposes your beautiful shoulders too."

Lea still wears her hair in a short sassy style, using a flat iron. Jessie has been growing her hair and as before, it reaches to the middle of her back.

Josh steps out to the courtyard in his black suit and dark blue tie. He looks so handsome and he seems almost smug, with his crooked smile. Sam is handsome and stunning in his long sleeved pink shirt, tan slacks and dark brown leather boots. I think to myself how confident Sam is to wear a pink shirt to his son's wedding, after not seeing his ex-wife in over thirty years. This makes me smile from within.

Dana Bea and I wear simple sun dresses, hers is the new halter style. I add a nice shawl over my shoulders.

The ceremony is quick, and intimate. They kiss and are introduced as Mr. and Mrs. Josh and Lea Rivera. This stings a bit for Sam, but he realizes he didn't raise his son and this honor should go to Juan.

At the reception, inside the winery overlooking the vineyard, Sam walks up to his ex-wife Michelle and says, "You are looking lovely Michelle." She bristles and replies, "Thank you Sam." I stand beside him and he introduces us. I put my hand out to shake her soft manicured hand, and say, "Nice to meet you." Jessie casually walks toward us and into a bee's nest. She happily says, "The baby is really kicking, can you see it Nettie?"

CHAPTER NINETEEN

Her comment is light hearted and precious, her excitement infectious. I catch a glimpse of Michelle and say, "This is my granddaughter Jessica, she and Lea have been best friends since kindergarten."

She shakes Jessica's hand and squeezes out, "Nice to meet you."

You could have cut the air with a knife. Why she is so hostel towards us is a mystery. It's her baggage, just let it go.

Jessie, looking lovely goes to stand next to her best friend Lea. Josh can't take his eyes off his bride. She is wearing a strapless white lace very tight gown. Her only jewelry is an opal necklace, a gift from Josh.

We sit at our table with family. Dana Bea looks lovely, smashing in her silky halter dress. The food is spectacular and the wine is flowing.

I keep looking at Josh and notice so much of Sam. It's a shame they lost contact. I put the blame squarely on Sam, he is the one who lost contact. I know how much he regrets this decision today. Just then Josh walks to our table to make small talk. He is very gracious, Lea is a lucky girl, if Josh has one cell that is from Sam, she will have a wonderful life. He kneels down next to Sam and they talk quietly. Sam stands up and pushes his chair back and tells us he'll be right back and follows his son.

He tells me later, they walked around the corner, grabbed some beers, two cigars and stood at the corner of the redwood deck, looking at the ocean where they poured out their souls. Josh was the aggressor and Sam apologetic. They have the same passion and are almost one in the same person. I have no specifics of this meeting, but when the two finally returned Sam was pleased, kissing me on the cheek. Josh grabs Lea and spins her around.

Archie stays close to Jessie and this is so sweet to watch. She is bubbling with pride and loves her belly. There are other girls from grade school who grew up with Jessie and Lea and everyone wants to share their journey into adulthood. Jessie happily introduces her husband Archie. Most girls reach out and rub her tummy and ask her when she's due. Some go so far as to ask how long she has been married. Jessica answers, "A week," she laughs, "No, it's been over a year." They ask where she met her husband and where they live. Lea looks at Jessie, they smile and understand this awkward feeling of idle conversation. Finally, Archie rescues her and they leave arm and arm.

We each go our separate ways, we have Charlie and Abby, so their parents can stay and party. We take off to the beach and chase the kids along the sand. They run around in the dark, running in circles and scream. When they are out of energy we happily put them back into their car seats and drive back to the hotel.

"Sam, I feel we have come full circle."

He looks at me with that smug look and says, "Be careful what you wish for darlin'." I lean over and hug his waist with my arms wrapped around him so he will never get away, while I feed my senses taking in his burly scent and whisper how much I love him.

Jessie and Archie stay as long as possible. She is beginning to fade and he is tired from a mix of his work and the flight. Dana Bea and Coach taste wines, dance to some slow songs then walk along the surf. She holds her heels in hand, with my shawl wrapped around her shoulders. Josh and Lea dance well into the night then fly off for a two-week honeymoon in Hawaii.

CHAPTER NINETEEN

Sam reminds me, "There's one more thing, Rich's sister Rose. Jessie might want to meet her, just out of curiosity, since Rich planted the seed that she looks like her. I have to wonder if that was his plan. Once a con, always a con." Sam has been stewing over this and feels better after warning me.

We give the kids a late night bath and get them tucked away in the other double bed. We collapse into the bed next to them.

"Goodnight cowboy, goodnight Tiger." We whisper to each other.

CHAPTER TWENTY

Bluebonnets

JESSICA IS IN LABOR, just as her doctor had said, exactly on her due date. It is uncanny how he knew the exact date. They drive to the hospital, Archie phones his parents, then us, we phone Dana Bea and Coach. It is a very long night, then morning. He keeps saying she is getting closer, closer, but no baby. I feel such compassion for her, but stay in the waiting room with the rest of the family. She and Archie want privacy and they have been taking birthing classes together to help with pain management. They are told that babies arrive on their own schedule.

Noon comes and goes, something must be wrong. We continue to pace and wait. Coach stayed back with the kids, which was a smart idea. Finally, the wide doors to the maternity ward fling open, out walks Archie, worn out, but his entire face smiles.

"It's a boy."

Jessie is resting, she had a pretty hard time and needs time to heal and catch her breath. Pretty soon they'll put their son in the nursery

CHAPTER TWENTY

so Jessica can grab an ounce of sleep. We hug and recall our own labors and deliveries—*women do that.*

Jessica is having no part of the nursery, she has her son brought back in, so he can lay next to her bed.

Sam stands and asks, "What's your big boy's name?"

Archie announces, "Speaking of big, he weighed in at 9 lbs. 9 oz. and he is 21 inches long."

All of the men croon, "Wow, way to go Archie."

We women say, "Oh, poor Jessie."

Archie proudly announces, "His name is, Samuel Cody."

His dad Ray jumps off his chair and gives his son a father son bear hug like no other, to watch this display of affection is a sight to behold, father and son rocking back and forth, and this rhythmic movement brings joyous tears to Archie's face.

Sam sits there waiting his turn to hug the new father and tears brim his eyes. He stands up, and walks over to Archie and shakes his hand, pats him on the back and declares, "Well done cowboy."

We women wait to visit our Jessica; she is the one who did all the work. Finally, the nurse walks out and says she is ready to take on visitors. Her mother-in-law Peg is the first to go in trailed by Ray. We let them be until they are ready for us to follow. They walk out, then Dana Bea and I rush down the hall, into her room, while Sam saunters along behind us.

She looks so happy, but pale. She has meds flowing into her arm as she is holds her son. "Boy, he is a big fella" Sam exclaims.

She takes the blue blanket off his head and proudly shows us his not so tiny feet and hands. He is as bald as a cue ball in a pool hall. He is sound asleep while we grandparents, and his Aunt coo and kiss his fat cheeks. Dana Bea whispers, "I'm glad it's her and not me," then squeezes my arm, we look at the each other and wink.

"Yes, it's a wonderful gift, the gift of life, and a long road to adulthood," I comment to whomever listens.

The new parents head home with their son the next day. It's not like it was when Dana Bea was born, mothers stayed in the hospital for a week after we gave birth, this rest period was shortened to three days in the '70s. Now, they pop out the baby and drive home.

Jessie is nursing and doesn't seem to have any trouble in this department, but she moves very slowly as if walking on egg shells. She also sits on a pillow. We women in her circle privately talk to her about this healing process, usually it's not so bad, it helps to sit in a warm bath. Dana Bea starts the water.

I coo to her, "But, dear Jessie, for your first child, you had an exceptionally large boy. Oh my little Jessie."

She hugs her son, kisses his head and says," Yeah, no kidding." And laughs towards Dana Bea who slowly nods in agreement.

Lea sends a bouquet of flowers and signs the card, "Congratulations, love Aunt Lea and Uncle Josh." Archie's office sends flowers and gift cards. They receive quilts, toys and many stuffed animals. Then the

CHAPTER TWENTY

stuffed footballs and basketballs began to show up. Someone sent them a stuffed bull, another gift is a cowboy hat, vest and chaps.

It's always comforting for family to circle around and share the love, but always better when they leave. Before we go, we deliver casseroles, gift cards for pizza, a container of freshly fried chicken, potatoes salads, breads and sandwich meats. I tossed in their laundry, and changed their sheets. Then Dana Bea and I fold clothes and put food away. We don't stay long, and frankly, it's time to go. I can plainly see she is exhausted and Archie also lacks sleep.

Archie and Jessica receive a long awaited letter from Cody. Archie opens the large envelope and out fall two letters, one addressed to his brother, the other one is addressed to Lea.

Cody has only praise for his new nephew and thanked them for including his name, he was very touched and repeated thank you a second time.

He writes, "He sure was a big guy you had there Jessie," and adds how anxious he is to meet him and toss some footballs.

He writes that he is in a hot spot and it is very dusty, dangerous and he wants out as soon as possible. He said the Army is not what he expected. "I'm glad I did this, I've learned so much about teamwork and brotherhood. I've finally grown up. I hope I make it home in one piece. Love you guys, and pray for me, Cody."

His letter has the flavor of sad undertones. In bed, Archie confesses how wrong it feels to be so happy while his brother is in such danger and enduring so many hardships. They hug and take advantage of any openings they find to sleep, each too tired to dwell on feelings.

Archie forwards the letter to Lea with a note he slipped inside, "We are doing great, come to Weatherford and meet our son one day when you two are able. But right now we are in dire need of sleep!
Arch and Jess."

Our ever extending family settles in for winter. Baby Sammy is growing and I personally think he is as cuddly and cute as a button, but he looks like a Sumo wrestler. He has a voracious appetite and Jessie is loving this process of motherhood. He is a bundle of joy, he has big blue eyes and has finally has grown some hair, or peach fuzz. Abby is in kindergarten and Charlie is learning so much every day in Elementary school. Sam and I are relieved we don't have to help him with his homework! Kids learn so much earlier than we did, and some of it is *high technology.*

One cold winter day the phone rings, it's Jessica in a fast whisper. I can barely make out what she is saying. I hear only bits and pieces. She tells me to tell Sam to phone Ray now and hangs up. Sam rings up his friend immediately.

Ray gives Sam the news, "Cody is severely wounded; he was shot in an exchange of gun fire, hit twice. He has been airlifted and transported to a hospital and already in surgery. It's bad."

Sam jumps in his truck and takes off to console Ray and Peg, and offer his support. I phone Jessie back so they know Sam is with

CHAPTER TWENTY

Archie's parents. Jessie is crying and so is Archie. I tell them I can't drive in the dark, they understand. I phone Dana Bea, Coach drops whatever he was doing and goes directly to Jessie's house.

Sam will get all of the details, everyone knows this. He will come back and fill us in.

Jessie sneaks into her bathroom and phones Lea. Lea answers and Jessie gives her the news. Lea gulps air and bust out in tears.

"No, not Cody, not Cody, NO!" Lea screams.

Her husband steps into the room, she drops the phone and he consoles her. He is mature enough to understand Cody was her first love and for many years. He also realizes that anyone fighting in any war is a hero and Cody has Josh's full respect. Jessie let's her grieve and wait for news.

It's a very long night of no sleep and mournful cries for Cody. We all suffer emotionally, the unknown is the worst; no one knows where he was hit, or exactly how many times, and worse—his prognosis. All we can do is try to be patient.

The next afternoon Ray phones Sam and lets him know what he has learned. Cody is alive and in ICU in Mirwais, located in Kandahar. He needs emergency surgery and there is no time to airlift him back to the States.

We are thankful he lives, but overwrought about his dire condition. We realize he is still at high risk and could bleed out. The horror of not knowing is the worst, and still no details. We here, in the States feel helpless. There is nothing we can do except function on a level of routine, hope and faith.

BLUEBONNETS

Cody continues to recuperate and heal. Two months later he returns to the United States. His injuries are revealed to his family after he is placed in the Veterans Hospital in Dallas, Texas. He is still in critical care and slowly begins to regain strength as the healing process continues.

He's endured months of antibiotics, blood transfusions and three surgeries to repair his thigh muscles and femur bone, and he has had extensive shoulder surgery. Sam can totally relate to his blown out shoulder and shares his sympathy in cards and flowers.

Lea talks to Jessie after she and Archie return from visiting Cody in Dallas. Seeing his brother so torn up is very hard on Archie. To witness his suffering, and know what his brother has endured these past months and before while in combat it agonizing for Archie. Lea asks permission to visit him too, just to tell him she received his letter and to wish him well. Archie shrugs his shoulders and Jessie thinks it might bring Cody out of his depression; you know, to see her face, even though she is married ... well ... on the other hand maybe not. They aren't sure if it's a good thing or not.

Lea packs her things and secures a hotel near the hospital and leaves to visit her first love Cody. Her husband Josh is okay with her doing this, he understands her connection and her love for Cody is strong— was strong—*was*.

Lea walks down the long hallway and turns the corner following the numbers on the rooms. She walks another length of hallway to the last room on the right. There lay Cody, his right leg hoisted up higher than

CHAPTER TWENTY

his left and is resting on a long pillow, his shoulder is in a sling, and he wears an eye patch. He turns his head and looks towards her as she enters the room.

Before he can speak, she says, "Cody? Oh Cody." And runs to him. Lea flings herself on him and engulfs his wounded body, she kisses his face. She tells him how very sorry she is for his injuries; she says how sorry she is for not waiting. He touches her arm and tells her he understands.

In a raspy voice he tells her, "I wasn't there for you either, I pulled away," deep breath, "I wasn't sure what to do with you. I needed time to grow up."

She tells him about her husband Josh, their home in Corpus Christie and all about her job. She leaves out some personal details, one being that Josh is Sam's son. She is careful not to rock the cart so to speak.

She lays down next to him and snuggles up to him real close and says sweet nothings. The nurse walks back in, checks his vitals and walks out, without saying a word. Cody puts his left hand on her thigh and rubs her soft skin and muscular leg. She turns towards him and kisses him on the lips. Then she slips her hand under the sheet. They lay together and relive the tender love they once shared for each other. She is gentle and hugs him as much as she can without hurting him. With his good arm he pulls her onto him, she lifts her skirt.

No one bothers this couple for a time, maybe they know when to stay away. The love between them is strong and passionate. She is confused and guilt ridden and tells him she's sorry.

He smiles and says, "You can stop by and visit anytime."

She tells him she didn't mean to lead him on, she is sorry and adds, "I can't do this." Tears bubble out of her eyes, she holds his hand up to her heart.

Then the nurse walks back in. Lea leaves the room and says, "I'll be right back."

He moans as the nurse checks his bandages and sling. She knows. Lea returns and waits for alone time, and tells him she must go, and gives him a tender kiss. More on the scale of a friend's kiss with hope. He squeezes her hand and tells her, "You're the only reason I stayed alive."

She says nothing and wipes tears away from her eyes, stands up next to his bed and holds his hand.

"You take care Cody; I will pray for your speedy recovery." She lets go and adds, "Maybe you should take a nap, sweet dreams," then walks away.

Cody does fall asleep and dreams of better days.

Lea doesn't phone Jessica or anyone else. She gets a call from Archie who asks her how Cody is doing, I mean, towards you? Lea said they had a very nice visit, he was very pleased to see me and I him. It was very healing for both of us. Her conversation is vague and odd. They share small talk then hang up.

Josh is happy for her return home, and they are in a good place. Life is good and they are looking to get out of their condo and buy a house. Lea has an appointment to meet with a realtor but has come down with the flu, so they have to postpone the search for their perfect home.

CHAPTER TWENTY

Two weeks later she confirms she is pregnant, approximately four weeks along. Her due date is early Fall.

Josh is over the moon. He phones his mom Michelle and both dads. Juan enthusiastically congratulates Josh and Lea. Sam is as happy as a clam. Whoopin' and sending good thoughts. Jessie hears about Lea's pregnancy from me, and wonders why Lea didn't phone her.

Archie does the math, looks at Jessica and she spouts off, "No way, she wouldn't! I wonder, I just have to wonder, what exactly went on at the Veterans Hospital, who does that anyway Jess?"

Jessie is at a loss for words, then thinks, "Now let's not turn something beautiful into a soap opera Archie."

They laugh "Well she does have a husband, maybe it is his."

Archie drives back to the hospital to visit his brother. The guys talk and then go to physical therapy. Archie helps his brother by being a spotter. For Cody this is the beginning of months of intense and painful physical therapy. It is a long workout and Cody works with all he has, he grunts and counts and strains.

"Hey Cody, I heard Lea came to see you, how'd that visit go bro?"

Cody puts the towel around his shoulder, wipes his face and without any emotion, "Great, she is great, and it was great to so see her again."

Archie reminds him that she is married to a nice guy, they work together you know. Cody responds with a defensive response, "Ok, and so …?"

Well, "Nothing much, just that she is pregnant, almost two months now? Archie, half-jokingly asks, "Bro, now when was it she visited you?"

Cody tells his brother, "Stop being a sissy butt gossip."

The brothers slap hands, and Cody shakes his head, puts the towel over his face, knowing the chances are high. Very high. Archie hears him murmur under his breath, his head under the towel, "Holy crap."

Word reaches Dana Bea, all family and friends. Now the waiting game begins. No one really suspects the baby could be Cody's. Impossible for that to happen, in a VA Hospital.

It's early fall and Lea is very large. She is uncomfortable and ready to get her body back. Her mother comes out to help and stays for two weeks. They all can't wait to see what it is, a boy or girl. Josh and Lea want to wait until it's born to find out.

Lea goes into labor as her water breaks in the middle of the night. The pains and contractions are close together and they are coming fast, seems like she has no time to mentally prepare. Josh phones Jessica to let her know. Jessie tells Archie and Archie phones his brother. No one is the wiser except this savvy trio.

Dana Bea knew Lea drove to Dallas to see Cody. She also does the math, but thinks, "Nah, he was in critical condition, could never happen."

Lea, her mom and Josh drive to the hospital; her pains are four minutes apart. She is admitted and prepped then put into a private room. She takes a deep breath and slowly lets it out. Josh phones Jessie with an update. Jessie tells Archie and Archie calls Cody.

CHAPTER TWENTY

The wide doors open to the delivery room and Josh suits up so he can be involved, he wants to cut the cord. Her mom and his mom are in the room also.

It's an easier delivery than Jessica's. Lea pushes for a half hour when she feels the head move into the birth canal, then one more big push and there it is, whatever it is, then another push and out pops a very large baby boy. Josh does his duty and cuts the cord and is ecstatic. Lea holds her son and looks as his face and his large stocky body. She and Josh kiss. Her mother holds her grandson, then hands him over to Josh's mother.

When the crowd leaves and she is alone, she phones Jessie, "It's a boy. His name is Cole Joshua."

Jessica thinks, "Interesting name, close to Cody."

"Oh, nice Lea, very nice name." Jessie happily suggests, "Send pictures."

Two weeks later photos arrive on Jessica's cell phone. Baby Cole is Sammy's twin. Cole has no hair, a large round head like Sammy, and big blue wide set eyes. Archie, comes in after work and Jessie asks him to take a look.

Archie walks in, picks up her phone and exclaims, "Oh my God, I wonder if anyone else will pick up on this, the boys look exactly alike."

"I know, I wonder if Lea notices, maybe it's nothing, maybe all babies look alike, let's not be mean spirited honey."

They don't tell Cody, but he hears the news from his dad Ray. His dad shows him photos that he got from Sam. "Handsome grandson you got their Grandpa Sam." Ray adds, "He looks just like his Grandpa Sam, and he sure looks like Archie's boy too."

This innocent statement from Ray goes over everyone's head, except me. Those boys have a distinctive look, Ray and both his sons have it.

I take Dana Bea by the arm and lead her outside, past the oak tree to sit on the swing. The two of us slowly move back and forth and hope no one takes notice and disrupts our precious time together. Sometimes it's nice to sit quietly and be alone with someone who is the same as you—*quiet*.

We silently admire the blooming Texas bluebonnets.

"Listen, it's the Meadowlarks; do you hear them honey?"

She nods, yes.

CHAPTER TWENTY-ONE

Nettie Reflects

MANY MOONS HAVE PASSED ACROSS MY LIFE, many loves, and disappointments. I lost my family then gained a family I think to myself, as I speak to Dana Bea, "I have broken the law and in doing so I have brought the best out of one beautiful woman."

I take her hand, and tell my daughter, "I have a wonderful daughter, you are always close by and I love you for giving me these beautiful grandchildren." Going on, "I also have a devoted husband who is my light." I quietly speak mostly to myself but aloud so my daughter can hear. "I am thinking a lot these days, about this situation with Lea. This obvious unfaithful deed towards Josh is between Lea and Cody. I'm sure Josh has no idea. He will figure it out one day, and yes, one day when the cousins are riding together and they jump off their horses and saunter up to the house. They will walk alike, they will be built alike, for they are identical. Yes, one day this falsehood will open up and unfold to expose what she is really made of. I don't want Sam to know, it will break his heart. Let's just put this one on the back burner shall we Dana Bea?"

"Yes Mom, let's."

CHAPTER TWENTY-ONE

Time passes and Cole continues to grow and fill out. He also becomes rowdy, but as sweet as pie. He is a quiet boy, but none the less, all boy. His cousin Sammy is just like his dad Archie was when he was a baby. His parents recall their similarities. No one mentions the fact that Josh and his son Cole don't look or act alike.

Both Sam and Josh have that crooked smile and a way of sashaying into a room. Cole and Sammy run in and roll out. Two husky playful boys.

The family is together for Easter break and the ladies are busy coloring eggs, and busy chasing off the kids so they can hunt them later with baskets. Company arrives, its Ray, and Peg with Cody.

Cody has a leg brace over his blue jeans, his arm and shoulder seem to be back to normal, but they never really will be quite the same. They walk in and everyone hugs and makes small talk. There is tension in the air. A stillness fills the once happy egg artists and hiders. Lea runs in chasing Cole and looks up.

"Oh, Cody, hello." She whizzes by chasing after her son.

Cody laughs and watches this scene. Josh walks over, snagging little Cole by the hand then introduces himself. They shake hands. "Here he is, here's my little guy." Josh picks up Cole and introduces him to Cody. Ray walks up and introduces himself to Josh as Sam's old buddy, and Cody's dad.

NETTIE REFLECTS

Ray looks at Cole and says, "This is the little guy I hear so much about. Ol' Grandpa Sam is sure in love with this one."

"I'm right here in the other room Ray and I'm not deaf." This results in a round of laughter.

Ray looks at Cole again, real close, intensely he studies Cole's face then he looks back at Josh, "Yes indeed, he is a fine boy Josh, you should be real proud."

I know Ray knows. He looks over at Cody and Cody pretends not to notice.

Cody keeps to himself and Lea does the same when she's not chasing Cole. Cody listens to Sam tell one of his wild Texas Ranger stories, then Ray jumps in and tells his version.

Jessie and Archie walk in from outside, their son Sammy runs past a room full of adults and jumps on Cole's back. The boys wrestle while Ray and Peg observe, "Seems like yesterday our boys looked like this. Yes, indeed, just yesterday." They are very quiet and watch, then look over at Cody.

"What? What did I do?" Cody asks with a suspicious voice. They don't answer, and continue to watch.

Josh brings in an armful of beers from the outside cooler and offers one to his Dad, Ray, Cody, Archie and Coach. The guys have a tall cool one while the boys play on the carpet in front of them. It's almost painful to watch. Josh and Sam don't seem to notice, but the rest of the room is on high alert.

CHAPTER TWENTY-ONE

Jessica helps me in the kitchen then Lea joins in. Dana Bea is with little Abby who is upstairs taking a nap. I suspect Dana Bea is more comfortable up there than down here.

Peg walks in and asks if there's anything she can do to help. Innocently I say, "Yes, you can help Lea fill the rolls then put them on a cookie sheet." Uncomfortable, the two-women work together, quietly. Peg is the one who breaks the silence.

"Tell me Lea, when was your son born, and how old is he now?" Lea answers Peg.

"It's so great to see all of you kids together again in the same house. Just seems like yesterday when you and Jessie and my sons were riding horses and having hay fights."

Lea responds, "Yes, just seems like yesterday."

Peg goes on, "I thought we'd lost our boy two years ago, you know, when he got shot up in the war. Didn't you visit him while he was in the VA Hospital Lea?"

I listen to this conversation and think, "Oh my goodness, Peg's going for the jugular."

No one dares interrupt. Dana Bea can hear everything from the staircase, she stays as still as a fly on the screen door. Everyone waits for Peg to go in for the kill.

Lea pops up with, "Well actually yes, I did visit Cody, when he was recovering from his wounds."

NETTIE REFLECTS

Peg chimes in, "It sure was hard to see him in so much pain. But he sure seems to have made a miraculous recovery these days."

Directly Peg asks, "Lea, when did you go to Dallas to visit Cody, may I ask?" She adds, "Were you carrying your son Cole at this time, or was it after he was born?"

Lea bristles and abruptly answers, "Before Peg, it was before he was born, why are you asking such personal questions, what is your problem?"

"Well, well, aren't you the snippy one," Peg says, then goes in for the slam dunk. Sarcastically Peg replies with her smooth as silk delivery. "There now, the crescent rolls are all stuffed and ready for the oven."

Lea takes off and gallops up the staircase, she nearly crashes right into Dana Bea.

"Ah yes, nothing better than a family get together at Easter time, and so many eggs ... " Peg sweetly comments.

The Easter eggs are colored, decorated, and the men hide them outside in the front and side yard. It's time for little hands to find them. The dads and granddads take all the kids outside and each one carries an empty basket. Lea stays upstairs while Josh goes outside with Cole.

Cody heads upstairs to see what is happening with Lea. She could hear him ascending up the steps from his uneven gait. Cody confronts Lea who is curled up into a ball, sobbing. He sits next to her and says her name, "Lea ... " She sits up, wraps a blanket around her legs for comfort and looks him in the eye and waits. Lea has no intention of starting this conversation, so he takes the lead.

CHAPTER TWENTY-ONE

"I know what is going on, everyone knows Cole is the spitting image of his cousin Sammy, and my brother, and our father and of me too Lea. He has the same face, wide set eyes, and same body type."

Peg calmly sits on the patio to watch the kids collect eggs. She takes a long drag from her cigarette holder. She deliberately blows the smoke out nice and slow and sexy. Her wheels are turning and Lea best get ready.

Lea sits frozen with Cody's straight forward honesty and blinks tears away. Silence fills the room as she stares out the window. They both know that time is closing in on them because it doesn't take that long to gather eggs.

She turns back to Cody, takes his hand and pleads, "I don't know what to do, please keep this between us, for me, for us—or do you think we should confess? I hate to pretend he is Sam's grandson, and not your dad's. I hate to pretend Josh is the father. I love it that he is yours Cody. I had no idea, not until he was born, but I knew the second I saw him."

Cody takes her in his arms and encourages her to focus on Cole, "Be the best mom you can be. Everything else will follow."

Lea and Josh return home the next day, but she never recovers from her continuous blue mood. She isn't feeling well. The next morning she packs up Cole and drives to the drugstore to buy a pregnancy kit. She takes the test and confirms she is pregnant, again.

NETTIE REFLECTS

Lea had been keeping her distance from Jessica due to guilt and shame. But now, Jessie reaches out to her friend, to support her through her unwanted pregnancy.

In late winter Lea brings another baby boy into the world. She names him Zachery Lee. This son has massive amounts of black hair and seems to have a crooked smile, or it could be everyone's imagination. He is lean with long scrawny legs. These little brothers, just sixteen months apart are polar opposites in looks. It is obvious to everyone; strangers even make comments. Lea is beside herself, depressed and suffers from lack of sleep. Mother Nature has revealed the truth. Her marriage has a fracture and there is a strong possibility it will get worse as time progresses.

Jessica announces she is pregnant and eight months later she delivers a baby girl. Her daughter is named Jana Rose. I think her daughter will be a healing process for Jessica. She will pile all the love she has been saving up and engulf her daughter, just as she does with her handsome son Sammy. Both children favor Archie, blonde hair, wide set blue eyes.

Grandpa Sam and I agree, it's time for some *us* time. We drive into a small town, enjoy lunch, sip wine and walk around the streets, go in and out of stores, the last one being an ice cream parlor.

We slowly drive back, clean up and decide to do what we do sometimes, and that is, we get real silly. We have not seen the kids, nor have we talked to them for a couple of weeks. Sam and I need alone time and adult conversation. Sweet Dana Bea unbeknownst to us has

CHAPTER TWENTY-ONE

been worried and missing us. This day, after Charlie goes off to school and Abby is in a day care, she drives to our house for some one on one adult time.

She quietly walks to the back of our lovely remodeled home and gently knocks on the door, I'm sure she expected to open the door and see us in bed with matching heating pads and Kleenex. She instead encounters a scene she certainly did not expect.

Dana Bea howls, "What are you doing?"

This intrusion causes me to jump, and smear toenail polish all over the end of Sam's big toe. There sits Sam with is big old long leg bent and his foot on my chair. "I was carefully painting his toes until you burst in." I smile and begin to remove the polish and clean around Sam's big toe.

I look at her and ask if she is okay and ask, "What brings you to our neck of the woods?" I giggle at that old slang and rephrase it with "… the flat dry plains surrounding us."

She laughs, "Well, I guess it *was* to check up on you two and your health."

Sam doesn't skip and beat and asks her, "You want your toenails painted?" He jokes and asks, "Do you have an appointment?"

Dana begins to laugh.

"I chime in and state, "Sam is an artist you know."

Dana Bea coolly asks as if this scene is normal, "Well mom, do you have any other color to choose from besides blinding neon red?"

I pick up a shoe box and place it on her lap, she rustles around in the box full of polish and pulls out a dark sexy maroon polish. "Well okay then," she murmurs.

Dana Bea slips off her sandals, scoots her chair in closer and puts her foot on Sam's chair. They laugh and Sam laughs out loud and says, "Ha, what a hoot this is, if only someone had a camera."

Ramona comes in with fresh cold lemonade to refill our glasses and returns with a plate of taquitos with salsa. She smiles and keeps her thoughts to herself.

Sam tells Dana Bea to relax as he begins to work his magic and paint her toenails. Sam declares, "Damn girl, I could land a helicopter on top of your big toe nail." She laughs out loud and continues to watch him paint. He smiles back and half looks up over his glasses with that ornery crooked smile.

I call the cooks to come back upstairs and in no time they bring up a second plate of beef taquitos. Dana Bea dips them into the guacamole. We have a great midmorning with flickers of light as the branches from the shade tree move with the breeze and the sun flashes through the Oak leaves from above. We listen to Sam strum his guitar while her polish dries.

CHAPTER TWENTY-TWO

Crossroads

JESSICA PHONES ONE DAY and asks if she can come over with the kids and spend the day. I happily chirp, "Of course, it's not a far drive and you know we always have food." Within two hours she arrives with her little boy and baby girl. Sam says he'll take little Sammy and check on the horses, then go into the old barn and collect eggs. Jessie says to her son, "You go with grandpa Sam to help." She keeps her baby girl close by.

As soon as the *men* are gone she says, "I am having turmoil in all directions Grandma." The most disturbing emotion is my dad in prison. I wish I had not gone there, and I wish I'd never met him, and I still hate him. But the another side of me feels grateful. I feel so conflicted. I feel love for him with apprehension mixed with disgust. He says I look like his sister in Yreka, her name is Rose.

I reply, "Rose, lovely coincidence."

CHAPTER TWENTY-TWO

"Yes, I was amazed when he said it, and Grandma, did I ever tell you my real birth date?"

"No Jessie, I didn't ask, but he told you?"

"Yes Grandma, my real birthday date is October 21, 1982."

I look at her and reflect, "Oh my Jessie, you certainly were a tiny little thing, Aunt Dana Bea and I thought we were giving you extra months because of your small size, but you were even older than we guessed."

We talk about this for a time, and I ask her if Dana Bea knows the date too, and she says with a big sigh, she is going to tell her everything about the visit one day when we have a break from raising kids. Then she jumps into her second cause for stress.

"Grandma, I have a dilemma. I have a problem; a deep problem I've been carrying around for a while and it weighs heavy on my heart."

"My secret will hurt a lot of people, like a domino effect."

"Jessie, do you need to talk to a counselor?"

"No Grandma, I need to talk to you because—I just do."

I take her hand and ask, "What is it child?"

Jessie answers, "I don't think Josh is Cole's father."

I look at her sweet worried face and don't have the meanness to say, *"Welcome to the club!"* I decide to wait and let her continue, get it out of her head and off her chest.

"I think, no, I know so, he looks exactly like Archie and our son Sammy and Cody, and their dad Ray."

Sitting quietly, the only sound is the screen door that slams shut, we both jump. I quickly whisper, "It's okay Jessie, it'll all be okay, don't fret about things you can't control. Remember this; oil always bubbles to the surface."

The birds begin to chirp and sing to us as we wait for our men to descend on the veranda. Our peaceful conversation is over.

"Sammy and Samuel, do you mind going downstairs to get some food and drinks?" On cue Sam knows we still need alone time and says, "Hey little fella, let's go downstairs and leave these ladies alone, this is just too girly for me."

Off they go into the back yard and around the corner. We take advantage of our time and I enlighten her to the facts that the cousins, Sammy and Cole do resemble each other, yes, those boys are nearly identical. I know you can see this, and I'm sure everyone knows too Jessie. "It's not a secret, except to Josh and Grandpa Sam."

"Lea's younger son Zachery is the spitting image of his father Josh." Jessie looks back at her wise old Nettie and smiles, and lets out a sigh. She is so relieved so I continue on to tell her, "Yes dear, this is a very touchy and sensitive subject and yes people will be hurt, and deeply."

CHAPTER TWENTY-TWO

"Remember, this is not our battle Jessie, you need to be involved with your little Sammy and daughter Jana. This situation with Lea, Josh and her sons is their situation. It is out of your control and it is removed from you and your marriage and your future."

"You focus on being a good loving wife and be supportive of Archie during this time. Focus on your own children and pray for Lea. God knows that girl knows how create a messy situation."

Jessie flings herself into my arms and we hold on to each other while we sit close together. We enjoy the sun streaming down across our intertwined bodies.

"Now to address your most concerning issue. Only you can cope with your dad, his history and his prison term. I think Sam can give you better advice than I on this. I just hope you will be very careful dear. His sister Rose might be very nice woman with a wayward brother, she also might have ulterior motives and use you as a pawn. This chapter could go in either direction. Tread lightly and think of your children. I'd advise you not to visit him with the children. Wait until you are not so busy and you are more able to handle what may come of this budding unconventional relationship."

We step down the creaking steps, I go on, "Now you and Grandpa Sam talk, tell him about your feelings and he will advise you and steer you in the best direction. I love you Jessie, you are a gem."

"Oh Jessie, let's not bring Grandpa into the Cole issue just yet, he is grandpa to Cole, but if Josh is not the father, then Sam is not related to him either."

"Oh right Nettie, I totally get that, thanks for the reminder."

Life moves forward and we still pad around the house with our red toenails. We listen to the kids and give advice. Play with the grandkids, and keep our rich relationships wide open with our children and their spouses.

Lea misses her family in California, especially her mother. I'm sure she needs the emotional support and trust. Her plan to live closer to her friends and Cody turned out to be a nightmare as Corpus Christie is more than a five-hour drive for her. She miscalculated the size of Texas. She is a young busy working mother with two rowdy sons, who are too close in age. Lea continues to stay in her marriage and Josh never utters a word about his first son, who is becoming the mirror image of Cody.

Cody has moved out from his parents' home and buys his own house, on the outskirts of Dallas, in a town called DeSoto. He continues to go to Physical Therapy three times a week and he continues to gain strength and balance in his life. I've heard that Lea visits him often. This is a subject I have to turn a blind eye to and let it go. Lea is caught between loyalty and love. She loves Cody deeply, and always has, and she loves Josh out of respect and marriage.

She can't make a move, she is scared and she doesn't trust her judgement any longer. So there she sits, in limbo.

Then there is Cody, who is trying to heal. Cody is taking classes at the local college. He is a busy man and ready to make his world a better one. Josh, he moves along through life as if nothing is amiss.

CHAPTER TWENTY-TWO

Dana Bea and Coach are happy and the kids are growing up fast. Charlie is very athletic, he is tall and thin, and resembles his grandpa Jim which makes me very happy. Abby is as cute as a button with a head full of dark unruly curls which I recognize all too well.

Jessica thinks of her dad and quietly dreams and yearns for his love, the love that was denied her when she needed him the most.

Today, Archie and Cody came out to the ranch to ride and recapture their youth. This is the second time Cody has tried to get back on a horse. This is bonding time and a chance for the brothers to get away and be free. It is a healing time and takes them back to simpler days. It is magic to see the brothers riding together across the plains with hooves kicking up dust.

Later in the day Jessica, Coach, Dana Bea and their children arrive. Josh pulls in about thirty minutes later with his sons. No Lea.

Sisters, Carmelita, Ramona and Marie, bring out paper plates full of fresh Mexican dishes. The budding cowboys; Charlie, Sammy, Cole and Zachery learn to ride, under the watchful eyes of two grandpas. Baby Zachery sits on his grandpa's lap, and off they go. Abby rides on her daddy's lap. All of our grandchildren are on a horse.

The next morning Sam and I sit under the Oak tree and listen to the wonderful stress free songs of the Meadowlark. It seems like a million years ago that I was happily married to Jim living a regimented life of comfort and unaware of any other way to live. Now here we are, me with my Sam; strong, tan and always ready for a joke or two. He is our family's heart and head of house. Everyone goes to him for advice. I never know what each day will bring. He is solid with his advice and tells the kids what they need to hear and no more. He is a straight shooter. His motto is: Be careful what you ask because if you ask Sam, you will get the truth.

The journey that led us to meet each other was as plain as a straight line that neither of us could see. He was there at the right time. Nothing with us was ever forced.

Our journey has taken us from the Golden State and beaches to the Lone Star State of long horns and wide open spaces, and oh the flowers along the way; the California Poppies and coastal ice plant, to the Texas Bluebonnets. Would I have done anything differently? Well, I wish I would have kidnapped Jessica weeks, months earlier than I did, to have saved her from the pain and torture she endured each day while I waited and pondered—finally, the idea grew strong, listening to her night after night—a child's screams.

I wish I'd moved quicker, faster, to reach Jim, just a second sooner is all I'd wish for.

I also regret the months I shunned Sam the first summer we met, I missed so many glorious sunsets with him.

Life is a potpourri of people who come and go out of our lives. I think to myself, back to younger days and deeply miss my sister Abigale and I surely do wish she had lived a longer, fuller complete life.

CHAPTER TWENTY-THREE

The Tables Turn

THE COMING YEAR LEA finally gains the confidence and nerve to step out of her marriage and leave Josh. Her announcement is painful and creates a long emotionally charged fire fanned divorce with money and custody issues at the forefront. She never confesses her oldest son is not her husband's. Josh is naturally hostile towards her for not trying harder to make the marriage work. He simply doesn't understand why, what he did wrong, and he has no idea how long she has wanted out. Lea on the other hand can't find a place to live fast enough.

She phones and confesses to Jessica, "Josh is a very nice man, he is a great boss and a wonderful father and friend. I just don't know what it is about him."

Jessie has to bite her tongue and not answer the obvious, "He's not Cody."

"In the beginning, being with an older mature man—a man who was my boss was exciting Jessie. Josh is handsome, honest and he loves me. But something has always been missing, and I hate to say anything

CHAPTER TWENTY-THREE

negative about such a wonderful person, but he bores me. I can't get him to ignite my fire. His stories are repetitive and his idea of fun is walking in the park. I need more Jessie, I need different, I need to feel more of an intense degree of passion." She goes on, "My boys are older, they run on a full tank of gas, they are so full of energy I feel as if I will lose my mind. I'm tempted to move in with Cody, but this will only add fuel to the fire and cause more pain for Josh. I don't want to insult him and well, play him for a fool. Guess I'll stay in Corpus Christi and continue to work and raise our sons. Josh keeps both boys every other weekend. Boy Jessie, I never thought I'd end up in this situation. I wish I had what you have. I should have waited for Cody."

Lea rambles on about her life and plots her next move, while Jessica politely listens. She loves her like a sister. She offers no advice because she wants to stay neutral. "I am so sorry you are going through such turmoil Lea, but I don't know how to fix this."

By the end of the year Lea can't stand it any longer and she asks Cody if she and her sons can move in with him. He is very polite but says he doesn't want that kind of negativity between him and Josh. "You are welcome to come over anytime Lea, but don't you think you should wait until your divorce is final."

She knows he's right, and lets out a deep sigh. He has never to this day asked her to marry him, but she doesn't seem to notice.

Jessica arrives at the ranch for New Year's Eve, Archie and the kids are already here, and Cody is coming out to join them. The cooks and I have a huge meal prepared and the drinks flow. They play games, kick back and enjoy old friendships.

THE TABLES TURN

I look at my family and remember the day I stood outside on my porch thinking to myself, tomorrow will be 1984. This scene played out so long ago, and look how our family has grown. Just then the phone rings, its Coach asking if they can come out for the weekend too, they could be there in two hours.

"Yes," everyone yells, "safe travels."

I ask Ramona to help get the other rooms ready and ask Carmelita to toss more food on the stove. Cody and Archie dart into the kitchen to pick at the foods already on the stove.

I announce, "Our family will again be all together to laugh, to toast to each other and bring in the coming year. It's been awhile since this has happened, we are so happy to have each one of you with us." We all raise our glasses and toast to family and friends.

I look over at Sam and whisper, "Boy oh boy Samuel, we're getting up there in age."

He smirks and answers, "Yep the only problem darlin' is this; no one's keepin' track," then slaps me on the bum. I exaggerate and lunge forward, then laugh on my way to the kitchen to go heat up more finger foods. I shoo the boys away from the cooks.

Soon there is a buffet table and the family can graze anytime they want. My mood changes when I realize Coach and family aren't here yet. I peek out the window and instantly think of my sister, peeking out, waiting for our parents' headlights. Panic consumes me, and chills run up my spine and cover me. I look back at Sam and ask him, "Please phone Coach." I tell him, "They should be here by now. Will you please do that for me Sam?"

CHAPTER TWENTY-THREE

Jessie asks, "What is it Grandma?"

Now the room full of partiers are quiet and looking at each other. I feel so silly, and sorry I am over thinking the possibilities, and playing old tapes in my head of years past.

Sam says hello, and I hear him tell Coach to be extra careful; lots of drinking and driving tonight. "Yes she is, yes I'll tell her. Okay, love you guys."

He hangs up, turns to me and says that Dana Bea knows what's up with you, and to please not worry, it'll be okay.

This evening is the longest in the world. The old Grandfather Clock ticks the night away, and with each second, it seems to tick louder.

The kids resume their games and I wait, peeking out between the curtains, making a bulge in the drapes. Time passes and I begin to weep, it's just too much. I know it's been too long for their trip. Ramona brings me a hankie. I wipe my face and blow my nose, I look back outside towards the long dirt road and sees two faint headlights. "They're coming!" I yell.

The family walks in and I run to my daughter and give her a hug, and the grandkids wrap their little arms around my legs.

Dana Bea encases me in hugs, and says, "It's okay, it's all good, now let's bring in the New Year."

She is gentle with her mom because she knows what triggered this panic attack.

THE TABLES TURN

The kids eat and the parents have a highball. Coach says, "Whew, talk about crazy drivers out there, you were right Sam."

I look towards Dana Bea, who smiles and repeats to her mother, "It's all good, no worries."

Jessica asks if anyone would like to try her new casserole she made for tonight. Archie yells, "Yes! Jessie, bring it on!"

She gets two potholders and carries in her first try at a Mexican dish, "It's called Chicken Molé."

"This recipe is a Mexican traditional dish for Christmas time. I cooked the sauce for days, it looks like taco sauce but you stir in dark chocolate, bits at a time, stir, then make sure it sits longer. Then, when it is ready, pour it over cooked cubed lean white chicken. Feel free to scoop it up with a tortilla. Lupe made the tortillas this morning," Jessica happily announces.

It smells delicious, Sam is the first one to scoop it onto his plate and take a bite. He chews the tender chicken and pretends to wince.

"Lord Jessica, are you trying to kill me?"

"What, what is it Grandpa, it is too tart, not enough spice, too much spice, or too sweet?"

"No little one, it is scrumptious, I just didn't want to die from shock." The family erupts in laughter and she promptly fills their plates. In the next room you can hear Ramona and Carmelita giggle.

CHAPTER TWENTY-THREE

The cooks, Carmelita, Ramona, Marie and their mother Lupe have begun to call me, *Abuela*. I love this name because it means *Grandma*.

Dana and Coach join in with the games while I tend to the little ones. The champagne flows and many stories grow into tall tales. They are all aware of Sam and his exaggerated stories, it's just like a Texas Ranger to tell a tall tale.

After the new year Jessie retreats back into a quiet withdrawal, sort of a mini depression. Sometimes young mothers experience this from low hormones. She finally gets the nerve to confess to Archie, that she has been mulling over her life and she needs to meet her Aunt Rose in Yreka.

"This is what I need to do Archie; *really*."

For some unknown reason, Archie understands her need, her vicious beginnings push her to make sense out of her life's journey. Archie is from a well-adjusted grounded family, but he understands her need to connect. Jessie needs to be complete.

He asks for a few days off, and on a Friday in February, they deliver the little ones to Dana Bea and Coach. I show up with Sam carrying a couple of casseroles and some fried chicken and wish them luck.

Jessie and Archie drive to DeSoto, to meet up with Cody, who drives them to the Dallas airport. They fly to Medford, Oregon, rent a car then

THE TABLES TURN

drive south to Yreka. An easy drive not far from Medford. Her highly anticipated journey is to find the key that will unlock her sadness.

She found Rose on the internet and phoned her in advance. She explains who she is and tells Rose that she has already visited her brother Rich at Pelican Bay prison.

"Yes, he called me after you left and told me about your wonderful visit. I am so pleased to meet you one day soon, and we'll drive over and visit with Gladys too."

This startles Jessie, "Who is Gladys?"

Rose is apologetic and answers, "Oh, I'm sorry dear, I thought you knew. Gladys, she is your grandmother, your mother's mom."

Jessie almost drops the phone. Long pause and she hears, Rose calling out, "Holly, are you there, Holly?"

"Ahh, yes, I'm right here Rose, ah, no, I mean I had no idea she was living or in your town."

Rose says, "Oh yes honey, your mother was born and raised in the house where her mom still lives." Jessie is speechless.

The drive to Yreka is more nerve wracking than driving to the prison. They pull up to Rose's address, study the house, there it is, a nice small nondescript home. Tidy yard with potted plants on the porch. They step out of the car, hold hands and walk down the sidewalk towards the red front door.

CHAPTER TWENTY-THREE

Archie tells her, "I'm right here for you Jess." They squeeze hands.

The meeting is as she expects. A bit uncomfortable, but also familiar, as if she has known her all of her life. Rose keeps referring to Jessie as Holly. Jessica finally speaks up and tells Rose, "My name is Jessica, Jessica Rose."

Rose apologies and repeats, "Rose? Who renamed you?"

"Oh, gosh Rose, I'd rather not say, but at the time she had no idea I had a relative who shared the same name."

Rose sweetly and proudly says, "Well isn't that something, Jessica Rose."

They have tea, and talk about Texas, Archie's family and his brother who fought in the war, and was wounded. They show Rose photos of their children and tell her their names.

Rose is so excited she blurts out, "Let's go meet your grandma Gladys."

The kids stand, take a deep breath and walk out the door. Rose says, "Jump in my car, I'll drive."

In no time they drive to a tidy cute farm house in need of yard work. This neglected house needs some care, that's for sure.

"This is the house where your mom was raised." Rose announces. Jessica's mouth goes dry and her face feels cold as she stares at the front of this house. Jessica feels conflicted, this is a woman, Gladys,

THE TABLES TURN

whose son-in-law is in a supermax prison and her daughter died from an overdose. Jessie is not sure what this family tree really means.

Rose reaches around Jessie and Archie and gives a familiar knock, then opens the door, walks in yelling "Gladys?" There in the living room sits a frail elderly lady with her walker next to her chair.

Rose says, "Gladys, this is your granddaughter, baby Holly." Jessie smiles and Gladys opens her arms and begins to cry as she says, "Oh my dear Holly let me hold you dear child."

Jessie steps forward towards a stranger, then bends down into the waiting arms of her grandmother.

Gladys reaches out with her skinny weak arm and takes Jessie by the hand. She says, "Let me look at you, what a beautiful woman you are, you look just like my Robin."

Jessie is speechless once again and looks back to Archie who has a look of shock across his face too. Jessica introduces him to Gladys and explains who he is and the story of flying out from Texas.

Gladys has many questions, she gets right to the point and doesn't hesitate, "Now dear girl, how did you end up in Texas?"

Before Jessie can answer Gladys says, "You know your mother loved you very much, but she was into drugs with that no good husband of hers, she died because of him."

Jessica follows Gladys' eyes and looks towards the mantle and sees a gold frame, a senior photo of her mother. "Yes dear, will you reach up there and get that picture for me."

CHAPTER TWENTY-THREE

Jessie studies it closely and says nothing, she can plainly see she is the spitting image of her mother, who also had long thick wavy hair. Nothing like the bleached out stringy hair Nettie saw. Her mother appears wholesome with her long waves and highly sprayed bangs. She wears a necklace with a gold unicorn. Jessie holds the frame and continues to study her mother's face.

Gladys goes in to great detail about her daughter's crush on this boy Rich. "They went everywhere, and she began to change by the time she graduated. She was so skinny and she was gone all the time. I don't know where they went, they were just gone. Her brother tried to spy on her for me, but she found out and they had a big fight."

Jessie asks, "Brother?"

"Oh yes, her brother Joe, he was such a nice boy.

"Was?"

"Yes dear, my son Joe was killed in action in 1983, in a place called Beirut. He died from a bombing at the Marine barracks, it was terrorists. They killed my Joe, and just a few weeks before he was coming home. He was so young."

Gladys points and says, "Over there, see his picture in his uniform." Archie steps up to the framed picture of her son Joe and looks at this face, the same face as his sister Robin.

"I'm so sorry Gladys."

She looks up, takes a Kleenex and wipes her eyes and says directly, "You can call me Granny."

THE TABLES TURN

This meeting is heartwarming, informative but extremely uncomfortable, for Archie too.

Rose comes out of the kitchen with hot herbal tea and asks, "Sugar or honey?" they both answer at the same time sounding like the Everly Brothers, "Honey."

Gladys asks her to please sit down on the ottoman by her feet. Archie sits on the end of the couch, Rose next to him.

The conversation comes and goes in waves, from their visit to Pelican Bay prison, to wanting to connect to her Aunt Rose and her Grandmother.

Gladys reminds her. "Call me Granny, please, I have waited so long to be called Granny, and to hear your voice. You are the answer to many prayers sugar."

Gladys tells Jessica that she has something for her to see, "It's my Robin's hope chest. It's lodged in the back of her closet, it's wicker, with two leather flaps to help lift the lid, you can't miss it. You go in and go through it, now don't be shy, and If you have any questions just ask … and you can have anything you want out of there too."

Jessica softly says, "Okay Granny."

Rose takes them to the back bedroom and they step back in time to the late 1970s, into what used to be Robin's bedroom. It is exactly as it was when she left home to marry Rich. Thumb tacks on a bulletin board hold in place; dried flowers that use to be a corsage, photos, and awards from her soccer team. Rose points and Jessica sees it; the trunk. Archie jumps in to help.

CHAPTER TWENTY-THREE

Archie pulls the wicker trunk out of the closet and they sit down on the blue shag carpet. He slowly lifts the lid. Staring back at Archie is a lime green chiffon prom dress, Jessie gasps with joy, takes it and puts the dress to her nose and takes in her mother's scent. She looks deeper inside and sees her mother's acid washed blue jeans, and a jeans jacket with buttons pinned all over the front and collar. Then she holds up a paisley skirt with pockets. She holds it close and feels something. She reaches into the side pocket and discovers a bracelet. It is inscribed, "Make love, not war." Jessie reaches for the Kleenex that Archie holds out for her. Rose walks back in and sits down on the bed and offers Jessica more information.

"Robin was a beautiful girl Jessie, and she fell hard for my brother. Rose darts out of the room with her hand over her mouth.

Alone, staring at a trunk full of a young girl's life, her mother's life, her hopes and dreams, Jessie looks at Archie and tells him, "I love you so much, thank you for coming with me."

Archie peers over the edge and looks, there on the bottom is a plastic bag full of photos, with a rubber band around it, and another bag that holds letters and drawings. Jessie sets the photos and letters aside and explains that she wants to look at them in private, back home while everyone is asleep.

She finds her mother's Strawberry Shortcake backpack, and she unrolls a poster, it's a photo of the Fonz. Another poster is wrapped inside the first, it is The Bee Gees and a third smaller one has a picture of a unicorn running with a rainbow in the background. She finds a framed photo in a paper sack along with a cassette tape of a singer named Phoebe Snow. Then she sees a cardboard box labeled *Holly*. Jessica quickly opens the box and peeks inside, there she spots folded infant

THE TABLES TURN

cloths, tiny pink leather shoes, and a jumper embroidered with the word *Cinderella* in pink thread. This task of unveiling a life full of promise lasts more than an hour. Gladys makes no sounds. They hear Rose drive back up to the house, she walks into the bedroom with pizza, then comes back again with sodas.

Jessie feels weary when she finds a soft fluffy pillow, the fur is hot pink with tassels on each corner. It smells of perfume, a scent called *Charlie*, she knows this because in the bottom corner of the trunk is the actual *Charlie* perfume bottle.

Finally, Jessica and Archie come back out to the living room and Jessica hugs her Grandmother around the neck. Gladys repeats, "Child, you truly are an answer to prayers."

Jessie keeps her head on her grandmother's shoulder and holds onto this woman who has suffered so much, and whispers "Oh Granny, thank you for everything."

Jessie asks a simple question addressed to both, her Aunt Rose and her Granny. Jessica clears her throat, "Were either of you aware that my dad beat me?" There is silence and an uncomfortable feeling in the air. Her Granny speaks up and answers this question.

"Yes dear, I heard something of that nature, Robin use to tell me she didn't know how to stop him. Robin called one night crying, *'He's going to kill her, he's killing her.'* But she would not let *anyone* help. We were helpless. Robin was afraid to leave him, he had some kind of hold on her. All I could do was pray for you."

Jessica, tells her new found relatives about a lady who took her in and raised her with love and a safe environment. Gladys goes on, "I didn't

CHAPTER TWENTY-THREE

know what to do. I just hoped and prayed you would survive I prayed, she must survive."

"I am so happy you came back and found me honey, and Rose is too."

Jessica and Archie listen intently as her grandmother tells story after story of her daughter's life. Aunt Rose is nervous and keeps herself busy, she brings in paper plates and hands out more slices of pizza and makes no comment.

Jessica decides not to reveal the scars that have never healed.

Jessie says, "My dad told me about the night I went missing, he said he carried me to this lady's house who lived down the street and around the corner. He placed me under a tree in about three inches of snow, then tossed a stick at the house. Sure enough, the lady stepped out of her house and rescued me. She said I was huddled up under the tree, she took me in, wrapped me in blankets and warmed me up."

She raised me. Her name is Nettie. These relatives are stunned that Robin agreed to this and amazed that Rich had the foresight to rid himself of his daughter, for her own safety.

Rose spouts out, "Good Lord child, you could have froze to death." she moans, "That boy never did have a lick of sense."

Gladys sighs and says, "We are all guilty. We let you down child, all of us, we knew it and did nothing. Robin wouldn't let us come around, she just told us to mind our own business, she wasn't the same person, was she Rose?"

THE TABLES TURN

Jessie jumps up and takes charge of the downward spiraling conversation, "It's all okay now, I'm fine, happy and I'm blessed. Let's continue on a positive note shall we?"

Then Gladys looks at Rose and says, "I just remembered something sugar." Gladys experiences a memory spark and says to Rose, "Check under the cabinet over there and see if we still have those home movies."

Rose checks inside this cabinet and tosses VHS tapes out onto the carpet and inserts one into the player.

"It's my Robin, see your mom Holly, as a young girl, a cute teen doing her favorite thing, which was cartwheels across the lawn, she used to do cartwheels all over the place."

There is a video of her in her formal, looking down as she watches Rich pin a corsage on her dress. Robin looks at the video camera and makes a silly face.

Out comes another VHS. "See there Jessie, see the couch, right here, Archie's sitting on it, see Robin's cute feet, her legs sticking out from under her paisley skirt, and now look sugar, there's Robin showing off her belly." On the video a pregnant Robin rubs her tummy and smiles at the camera. "That's you Holly."

For Jessie to see her granny's couch, and watch a video of her daughter pregnant on the same couch is extremely important for this wounded grandma.

Jessie holds onto Archie's hand that lay for support. "Next is another video of my Robin, she is here at my house, this house, it's the same

CHAPTER TWENTY-THREE

couch, see? See how peaceful she is as she sits on the couch holding you in her arms, see Holly?" Rich stands next to her, holding a cigarette and a beer. Halloween décor is behind them. Jessica is captivated by this visual.

Gladys asks where they are staying and Archie tells her about the motel close to the freeway. She offers her house, but they decline as their luggage is already at the hotel and they have to drive back up north to Medford early tomorrow morning to fly home. Jessie jumps in and says, "Our kids are waiting for us."

Granny orders, "Jessica, please take this wicker trunk, put it on the plane or you can take it to the post office, and you take the videos too honey. It will make me more than happy if you take your mother's senior picture too, I have stared at it and cried long enough. It's time for you to have a piece of your mother dear child." This unexpected generous gesture caused Jessica to lose it, she burst into tears, blows her nose and tells her Granny thank you and gushes that she loves her.

"Honey, may I touch your hair?"

Jessica replies, "Yes please do."

Jessica sits down on the carpet next to her Granny's chair, she puts her head back. Gently and softly her grandmother touches her long waves, she pulls her aged fingers through her golden curls and smiles. Her Granny pulls it back into her hands as she must have done so many times with her daughter Robin, as if she is going to make a ponytail. Gladys pats Jessica's hair and tells her thank you.

THE TABLES TURN

Jessie looks over to Rose and says, "You and I haven't had much time to reminisce, but I am so proud to have you for my Aunt, and I am so proud my middle name is same as yours."

Buckets of tears are shed, but Jessie and Archie need to stay ahead of the schedule and make their way back to their hotel. They decide to leave before 4:30 P.M. so they can hit the post office and ship the trunk home. Rose lifts up the leather flaps and drops the tapes inside, Robin's senior photo, frame and all, wrapped in the morning paper. Rose grabs some family table cloths and a picture from the kitchen Gladys had set aside.

Gladys, says, "Yes, put those in Robin's trunk too."

Rose jumps up and says, "I'll drive you to the post office Archie, I know this town like the back of my hand."

This moment is not about meeting strangers who refer to her as Holly, this moment is about family, and her Granny who waited a lifetime for this moment. Jessie promises she will return with her son and little girl one day, and her Granny asks, "What are the names of my great grandchildren Sugar?"

"Our son is Samuel, and our daughter is Jana Rose.

"Oh, I love their names."

Rose jumps in, did you say her middle name is Rose?" Rose has to run out of the room and blow her nose.

CHAPTER TWENTY-THREE

"Thank you Holly."

Jessie whispers to Archie, "Oh dear, she keeps calling me Holly, she forgets my name, oh well, in the large scheme of things, it really doesn't matter. Besides, it's been a long day with lots of stories and surprises for everyone"

Archie tells her, "She didn't forget your name, since your birth, to her, you are Holly, her long missing granddaughter, lighten up Jess."

Jessie spends weeks sorting through her mother's letters and photos. Then one afternoon she puts everything neatly back into the trunk and slowly comes out of her depressed state. She phones her Aunt Dana Bea and her Nettie and explains what she's been up to, and thanks them for giving her space.

CHAPTER TWENTY-FOUR

Old Friends

RAY CALLS SAM and suggests they have some old Ranger fun. Ray tells Sam the good news about his son Cody. He is working these days, he received his degree and has been doing student teaching this past semester. He landed a teaching job, and he'll be full time, with health benefits, besides his VA benefits. Cody continues to improve every day, with lots of hard work outs and much pain, he is coming back. He finally is able to have his eye patch removed. He can see fine, but wears glasses, and with thick dark frames, he looks like Clark Kent.

Sam shouts, "The hell he does Ray."

Ray happily replies, "He will be teaching Spanish at DeSoto High come fall."

"Great news." Sam happily says and adds, "I'm so happy for that kid. He surely has suffered with dignity."

CHAPTER TWENTY-FOUR

This call, asking Sam if he can come out to the ranch for a visit isn't about Cody. Ray has a lot more on his mind than a simple visit. He wants to talk to Sam about Josh's oldest son Cole. They set a date and hang up.

Late one morning, Ray shows up as scheduled. He parks way down the road, under one of the trees that line the old fence. Sam opens the creaky wooden screen door, yells and waves him in. They sit and have coffee and zucchini bread The eat and talk, but both seem anxious to get outside and have some *guy time.*

"You want to take a walk?" Sam smiles and without saying yes or no, they walk out the back door together. They take off down the long dusty road and talk about their lives, sore muscles, kids, money and shooting skills, Sam's ankle and Ray's back. Then Ray clears his throat and gets up his nerve. He is a straight forward kind of man and doesn't mince his words, he just spits out whatever he is feeling. True to form and right out of the blue he states his suspicions, "Sam, Cole is Cody's kid, and I hope this observation doesn't cause a wedge in our friendship." Ray goes on, "I have admired you and liked you for more years than a guy can remember."

Sam keeps walking with his head down, he listens with no interruptions. Then there is a lull in Ray's conversation. Sam just keeps on walking, not really thinking about his comeback, but mostly to push Ray's buttons. They walk and walk and Sam kicks some dirt balls and coughs.

Sam finally clears his throat and replies in a low matter of fact voice, "Hell Ray, I know Cole is your grandson. I've known this since the day he came home from the hospital."

OLD FRIENDS

"Ray looks over to his friend and Sam returns the gaze. Ray notices Sam flashes his crooked smile.

Ray says, "Oh hell Sam."

Sam slaps his friend across the back and says with a chuckle, "Now go get your grandson and bring him back here to spend the weekend, and let's teach that boy and little Sammy how to ride."

"Do you think Josh knows Cole is Cody's kid?" Ray needs assurance.

Sam looks at his friend, "Ray, Josh would have to be a moron not to know, but then again, I didn't raise him." The two friends get a good chuckle from Sam's quick comeback. Both men continue to walk and moan. "Oh hump, hell no, he has no idea."

Sam stops dead in his tracks, looks at Ray and asks, "How the hell did he do it, Cody I mean, not to get personal or anything, but hell Ray, he was all shot up and gets Lea pregnant! Hell Ray, he must be the bionic man." They walk along laughing about Cody who still in ICU pulled it off, "… you know, sex and all."

Sam gets serious and says, "There is no problem with our friendship Ray, what happened between them may have happened more times than we know or want to know.

They sniffle a bit and shake their heads then Ray agrees, "I don't even want to know."

Sam chimes in, "Yeah pal, let's not even go there." They belt out a laugh.

CHAPTER TWENTY-FOUR

Then Sam blurts out with a loud voice, "Oh my glory!" Both friends walk along, silence is golden.

Then both men, at the exact same moment reach back to their jeans and in slow motion, they take their guns out of their holsters, stop, neither moves a muscle. They slowly and with purpose raise their guns and begin to shoot rapid gun fire at the same time.

When the dust settles, "Oh hell Ray, did you see that, I shot him right between the eyes, I blew his damn head off, and with my left hand, ha!"

Ray yells back, "You are blind in one eye and deaf too, you hit the dirt six times Sam!"

They laugh a good long laugh then each gingerly step closer, Ray bends over, gets a stick and flings the dead rattler into the ditch.

"Remind me on the way back to bury that mean ol' snake's head," Sam orders.

Sam and Ray continue to walk the fence line, following along next to the dry ditch, they sprint across to the other side, walk cautiously towards a lone weathered tree. There they spot a rope dangling from this old oak, swinging in the breeze. On the end is the enemy. Slowly they pull out their guns, crouch down and prepare to blow away a burlap bag full of sand. Sam reaches out with his arm to use as a level and puts his gun over it to help him aim.

Ray yells, "Mother cracker!" Both unload their guns into the bag.

Sam is laughing so hard he can hardly speak. "Did you just yell mother cracker?"

Ray yells over the wind, "Yeah, I was overwhelmed." They slap each other on their backs while the tattered bag slowly swings back and forth spilling sand out from multiple bullet holes. The Rangers retreat and slowly walk back towards home.

They stop halfway down the road to lean on the old rail fence to shoot at squirrels and some sage brush. Sam hits a tumbleweed and it explodes, he yells, "Mother cracker" and they howl at the moon.

Ray yells real loud above the wind, towards Sam, "You still got it Grandpa."

"You too Grandpa."

Sam crouches down and Ray squints to see what his friend sees, then Sam stretches out his left arm for balance and lays his gun across his outstretched arm and shoots a dangling piece of wood swinging from the roof of the old tractor barn.

"Oh hell Sam, shoot something worth killin'."

Ray crouches down and points towards the barn and shoots a soda can off the back of an old rusty tractor fender. He shoots and clicks off a full round until it can't move.

Sam laughs and tries to speak, but chokes instead, then finally yells, "You killed it, you mother cracker, you killed my favorite soda can, you old sniper humper!"

CHAPTER TWENTY-FOUR

Sam finds his composure and says, "… probably better get back, I can smell dinner from way out here. You want to stay and have something to eat?"

Ray happily says, "Hell yeah Sam, that Carmelita is a hell of a cook."

They say nothing, just two old pals walkin' along out in the middle of nowhere and smiling to themselves, and shaking their heads.

The lightning comes out of nowhere, followed by deep rolls of thunder. In no time the rains fall in buckets, here and there, but not everywhere, but it does land on their heads as they limp along and try to pick up speed. The men keep walking a brisk uneven stride and never look at each other. They head to the back door and instantly I hold the door open, and hand them two large towels to dry off. They kick off their boots, and I order them to step out of their clothes and I toss them into the dryer.

Ray chuckles, "Thank you, I think." They laugh like two drunken wet sailors, which brings on snorts. They saunter into the kitchen, each with a bath towel wrapped around their waist and soggy dirty socks.

Carmelita watched them walking down the road. She prepared some spicy scrambled eggs with peppers and sausage diced nice and small, she wraps the eggs into a freshly made tortilla. She walks in and says, "Desayuno burrito."

Here they sit, two former Texas Rangers in dirty socks and bath towels, hunched over their plates gobbling down magnificent breakfast burritos with spicy salsa on the side. Not a care in the world.

Ray yells, "Gracias!" into the kitchen.

Carmelita pops her head around the corner, giggles and replies, "De Nada."

They are cold but happy. I come back in and toss them each a long sleeved t-shirt to slip on and add, "Everyone in the house watched you two walking down the road in the rain."

No reply, just a crooked smile and a sheepish Ray.

Ray takes another bite and leans into Sam and whispers, "Mother cracker."

They begin to snort again and belly laugh like two little boys. They inhale the food, as the storm blows over. I hand them their folded dry jeans and shirts so they can redress.

Sam walks with Ray out to his car, still parked way down the road, and says, "Been fun Ray, why the hell did you park so far down the road, anyway?"

Ray just shrugs, and quietly lies and says, "Best tree for shade."

They turn down the long road and walk towards his pick-up truck, no need to talk. They walk along and kick at a few rocks as they lumber along; lifelong pals who will forever share a grandson.

CHAPTER TWENTY-FIVE

Turn of Events

LEA STILL LIVES AND WORKS IN THE GULF AREA, and yearns for Cody, she still pines for him, and feels cheated in life. Josh and Lea share custody and have an agreeable platonic existence, living in the same town and all. Lea found part-time work so she can earn her own money and raise her sons. She never did become a teacher; it was just not her calling. But she always manages to land on her feet.

Dana Bea stays busy with raising her children and going to the high school games to watch and support Coach and to little league games to support Charlie. They both miss the climate on the California coast, but know they are in a great financial place and find other ways to cool off.

Jessica and Archie are in a very comfortable place in their marriage, raising Sammy and toddler Jana, they talk about trying for baby number three one day. Sam and I are getting up in age, but thankfully we have not lost any marbles. All of the kids still come to visit, ride horses and collect eggs while I fret over the little ones. Sam never

CHAPTER TWENTY-FIVE

changes and loves the company who still enter through the back door and stay all weekend.

But, change is in the air, and it is going to mix up the family and catch most of us off guard. This coming event will be a true test of loyalty.

Just as I predicted, there is going to be another wedding at the ranch. This time the bride and groom will be Ramona and Hector. Their grandmothers, mothers and aunts prepare the dishes, while Ramona and Carmelita and their sisters, Josie and Marie rush about to prepare for the festivities.

Cody and Archie help move equipment; Hector tells them where to park everything. Hector has been busy raking and pruning and preparing for this day. Cody is busy pushing bales of hay to the side and dusting tables.

This wedding is much different from the others. For starters, Ramona has fourteen bridesmaids and Hector has fourteen groomsmen who will proudly stand up for them. There are many well-wishers, family and too many small children to count. Sam looks out the window and asks me, "Is this is a wedding or a reunion for the entire country of Mexico?"

I smile and say, "Oh Sam, you know their culture, it's all about family—a very large family."

We sit with our own family, Dana and Coach and kids arrive as do Jessica and Archie, Cody and his parents are there too. Lea didn't come up as she has the boys this weekend and it's such a long drive.

TURN OF EVENTS

The music is played by the same Mariachi band, which makes me remember my own wedding. The sounds are happy and fill the air with joy. Ramona looks wonderful in her long white lace dress; her long thick black hair is pulled back to form large curls on the back of her head.

We dine on the best of foods with seasoned cooks coming from all over the state. This is a sight to behold and smell. One can only imagine this buffet line, the intoxicating smell steams and wafts out and up into the sky.

Hector wears a white suit, something none of us had ever seen him wear. The boys are shocked. He also sports a white cowboy hat. He looks so handsome, scared and uncomfortable. Archie asks Hector if he is going to stand on top of his wedding cake after his marriage. Hector laughs out loud, and yells, "¡Pierdete!"

Archie and Cody pat his back and the three friends since childhood have a good laugh. I'm sure he wants to get out of that three-piece suit with a bow tie this minute.

Once they kiss and walk between the line of twenty-eight members of the wedding party, the photos take another 45 minutes. No time to worry about the well-wishers. Everyone is supplied with shots of tequila, and cigars are passed around .

Carmelita is her sister's maid of honor. She looks lovely in a bright yellow satin dress with a Spanish shawl with a floral design. She walks over to our table and asks how we are doing and if we need anything. Sam tells her, "This is Ramona's day, we can manage. You look like a princess Carmelita, don't worry about us darlin'."

CHAPTER TWENTY-FIVE

She lingers for a minute or two, then responds with, "Gracias."

The music begins, an hour before midnight. This is going to be a long one. Ray and Peg head to the dance floor along with Archie and Jessica. Cody looks around and grabs Carmelita—everyone dances.

Dana Bea asks us if we'll keep an eye the kids so she and Coach can dance too. Grandpa Sam heads to the barn with his grandsons. I get little Abby all to myself.

The kids are falling asleep on blankets we had laid out on the grass, and most of the little kids from Hector and Ramona's families sleep along side our little ones.

I tell Sam that I'd give anything to slither down and sleep with those sweet kids. He holds my hand and says, "Hang on Grandma, we'll have lots of time to sleep long after this day is over."

One by one the parents scoop up their children into their arms and walk to their cars. This includes our friends who drive home, and our family who walk towards the house to disperse into different rooms. Sam and I walk together towards the back of the house to our private casa and drop like two heavy bricks onto our bed.

Ray and Peg stay here along with Cody. By the way, where is Cody? No one has seen him and there are so many beautiful girls to choose from, we decide he is a big boy, let him have some fun.

TURN OF EVENTS

Lea shows up two weeks later. Cody is polite but aloof. Jessie asks Lea if she called first or did he invite you to come and stay with him? Lea said, "Well, I didn't know I had to make an appointment, after all, I'm bringing his son so they can have a relationship."

Jessie carefully cautions her friend, "Lea, it doesn't work like that, you can't use Cole as fish bait!"

The girls get into a pissing match when she replies, "Is this what you think I'm doing? Do you think this is a game?"

Jessie now has the confidence to defend herself and answers, "I think you think it is, you are pushing too hard Lea, give him some room to come to you."

Lea responds with, "Thanks for nothing." She slams the receiver down with a thud.

A month goes by and Jessie finds out she is going to have baby number three. They are thrilled and tell everyone in ear shot. No word from Lea.

Cody shocks everyone when he phones his brother and tells him he's getting married. Archie says, "Seriously bro, this is great news, and it's about time, when are you two going to tie the knot?"

Cody is very quiet and in a soft voice says, "In two months, but it's not Lea."

CHAPTER TWENTY-FIVE

Archie looks at Jessica who listens to bits and pieces. He says to Cody, "Hang on." Archie puts his hand over the receiver and says, "Cody is getting married." Jessica's mouth drops open. He goes back on the line, "So yeah, wow bro, big shock here, does she have a name, or is it just, *lucky girl.*"

Jessica punches Archie in the ribs and he groans. He says, "Hold on bro, Jessie is beating me up." He looks over at Jessie and says, "It's not Lea." Jessie's mouth drops open again. She begs, "What, who?"

Archie listens and his face shows no sign of life as his brother fills him in with more information. "Yes, for sure I'll be your best man, yes bro it will be an honor. Okay, yes no problem, you call Dad and Mom and let me know when you tell Sam and Nettie. Your team of spies here in Weatherford are on your side, and our lips are sealed." And adds, "Team Cody over and out."

Jessie is on the couch next to Archie, bouncing up and down on her knees. Sammy playfully reminds his mommy, "We're not supposed to jump on the furniture mommy."

Sammy grabs some cookies and runs into the family room.

Jessie laughs and grabs Archie by the collar and says, "Tell me!"

"Jessie you cannot utter a word to anyone. Lea doesn't know and she is going to blow a cork, seriously, you will be able to hear her scream all the way from the gulf and then some."

"Archie, tell me."

TURN OF EVENTS

Cody is engaged and has been for a while, they have kept in on the down low until the time felt right, or safe.

"Who is it?"

Archie looks at her and says, "Carmelita." Then goes on to say, "My dad is going to flip out, he loves her cooking!" Then lets out a laugh, "Ha, dad always thought Lea was a pain in the ass."

Jessie yells, "Archie!"

In the days to follow their phone continues to ring off the hook, first me, then Sam, then Dana Bea. All are trying to absorb this exciting news, but in some way, this news surprises no one, although no one suspected it to be Carmelita.

When did this happen? Cody opens up a tiny bit about their journey and confesses that when he was in the hospital Hector drove Carmelita and Ramona to the VA hospital many times.

Jessie interjects, "It's a blessing they didn't run into Lea during her visit, if you know what I mean."

Archie says, "Way to call it potty mouth."

This makes Jessie laugh out loud. Archie goes on to explain, "Their relationship happened slowly. When they came to visit and cater to him, Carmelita always offered him homemade food. She also wrote to him while he was away during his stint in the Army, and he always wrote back to her. She has had a crush on Cody since we were kids. And yes, she knows about Cole. Cody is going to call Lea tonight."

CHAPTER TWENTY-FIVE

Lea, the score keeper, has been counting how many days it has been since the last time Cody phoned her. She suspects he is avoiding her. Fuming inside her head, she waits. When he phones, she is all over him with insults. She tosses in her sons and her job into the mix to make herself a victim. Cody listens, a quiet man, he waits his turn, then responds with the facts, "I've met someone, actually," he explains, "she is someone I have known for a while."

Lea is livid, she begins to yell and cry, then pulls the ace card and mentions their connection—Cole. "He doesn't even know who you are Cody!" She reminds him of their love and all the years she has waited, and reminds him she left her marriage for him, and continued to spew out her anger.

Cody listens then calmly announces, "Lea, it's over between us."

She screams and starts in again, but before she can lash out more anger he interrupts and informs her of more news.

"Josh and I have a meeting later this week, he knows the truth and I am asking for visitation rights."

Lea states, "Over my dead body!"

Cody calmly informs her that he had a DNA test a month ago with Cole. Josh agreed to this and told me he had always suspected. Lea is silent, he can hear her breathing heavily into the phone, followed by sniffles then she calls him, "Scumbag."

Cody quickly shoots back with, "You should talk."

Lea, taken back, gets serious and calmly informs him, "Cody, this is my choice, my son, and my judgement call."

Cody reminds her she lost her judgement call when she slipped into his hospital bed. He continues, "Cole is my biological son, Josh is his legal parent, this will be worked out with legal counsel no matter what names you call me."

Well, this conversation isn't going to end well, but he doesn't care, he is over her. His only thoughts are of a dark skinned beauty who has a heart of gold and patiently waits for him. "Goodbye Lea."

Lea phones Jessie and asks for information, "Yes, I just heard about this last night." Jessie confesses.

Lea boldly states, "And you didn't warn me, who is he seeing?"

Jessie coolly replies, "It is not for me to name names, ask Cody."

Lea pleads, "I can't do that, we aren't speaking, I'll phone Nettie, she tells me everything."

They hang up the phone. Jessica hits speed dial and beats Lea to the punch. She prepares me, then quickly phones Dana Bea to warn her too. No one is going to give Lea any details. This is Cody's time, and we also want to protect Carmelita.

CHAPTER TWENTY-SIX

Father's Unite

JOSH AND CODY MEET FACE TO FACE so Cody can show him the paperwork, in person with lab results from the DNA test, they have a nice long talk. Josh calmly admits he knew it all along. He confesses to Cody, "It was obvious when early on he began to look like you, not me—*very early on.* I tried so hard to please her and pretend she didn't cheat and I prayed it wasn't true."

Josh looks straight at Cody and said, "I am truly sorry about all of this, but, then again I'm not. "I don't want a wife who will cheat on me and not be a truthful person about the child I assumed was mine."

Josh and Cody decide to meet with an attorney to help sort this out. Josh tells him, "I'll make some calls Cody, and congratulations buddy." They shake hands and Josh drives back to Corpus Christi.

CHAPTER TWENTY-SIX

The wedding day is only two weeks away. Their ceremony will be much different from all the weddings at the ranch, this one will be held in Cody's parents' backyard, very private with immediate family only. Carmelita tells her extended family there has to be a cut off in this line of many loved ones. She will have only one attendant, her sister Ramona. Cody will have his brother Archie stand next to him. No date of the nuptials is announced, and no one informs Lea. The families on both sides plan for a huge reception at a later date.

The day arrives and Josh delivers Cole to Cody's house, then takes his little son Zachery for a play date, alone just the two of them.

Jessica, Archie and little Sammy arrive early for the ceremony. Jessica feels queasy while Archie looks smashing and happy. Jessica left Jana with her Aunt Dana Bea and Coach. Jana was overjoyed to play with her cousin Abby for the day.

Sam and I stay home to be polite and not be wedding hogs. We decide it wouldn't be fair to Carmelita's side of the family. Ray and Peg are over the moon with joy, they have loved this girl he has fallen in love with for many years. Peg steps forward and announces that they arranged to have the food catered. "This is Carmelita's wedding —no need for her family to prepare the meals, it's their ceremony too."

The only music is a cello, there are less than twelve guests sitting in chairs, and few children. Archie steps out in a long sleeve cotton shirt and tie, cotton dress slacks, Cody wears a suit. The brothers stand together and wait. Out walks Ramona wearing a cocoa colored sun dress, the combination of the dress with her dark skin and her hair pulled back, is exotic. Hector stands in the back and can't take his eyes off his new wife. Then the sliding door opens and out steps Carmelita, wearing a white dress to her knees, white heels, and a small thin net veil that covers her face. Her thick black hair falls in a cascade of curls flowing down her back.

Their ceremony is quiet, intimate and soulful. They have a priest and the ceremony moves rather slowly. Finally, the priest pronounces them man and wife. Cody carefully lifts her veil to reveal her dark brown eyes and beautiful face, he slowly and with purpose folds the netting back onto her head, he brushes away her tears that slowly fall down her high cheekbones, she sparkles with joy and love. He gently kisses Carmelita, then takes her hands and lifts her arms up above her head and announces to the guests, "Mi hermosa esposa."

Everyone stands up and claps, and take turns with hugs. Each guest has something special to say.

Cole sits with his grandpa Ray, who takes his hand and walks him towards Cody and Carmelita. Little Cole is wearing the smallest suit in the world. They walk to the couple and Cole tugs on the tale of Cody's jacket and asks, "Are you my daddy?"

Cody squats down and tells his son, "Yes big boy, I am your daddy, for ever and ever."

He picks up Cole in his arm and gives him a hug and adds, "I love you little buddy." Then sets him back down onto the lawn.

Cole is a chatter box like his grandpa, he looks up towards Carmelita, and asks, "Hi Car-me-lota, do you remember me, my name is Cole."

She squats down to be at his level, she looks at this small boy who looks exactly like the man she just married, this little boy who can't pronounce her name. She smiles and pats his hair softly and holds

CHAPTER TWENTY-SIX

his face in her soft gentle hands and softly says, "Si, chiquito." Cody smiles and offers his hand to help her up. Cole is happy and runs off to play with his cousin Sammy. Cole and Sammy play into the evening.

The party lasts a few hours, just enough time to eat and visit. Then everyone tosses rice while Cody and Carmelita dash down the sidewalk to their waiting car. Archie and Jessie dash to the car, laughing and tossing rice. Cody and Carmelita jump into the back seat like celebrities. Everyone smiles and laughs as they are chauffeured to the airport. Cody takes his bride to San Antonio for their honeymoon. A city she has always dreamed of visiting. They stay in a plush hotel at the end of the famous River Walk, not far from the bridge. They eat in an open air patio, and take a boat ride in one of the tourist boats which slowly moves along the River Walk. The river has stores and bars, restaurants and patios and hotels that line either side. They visit the Alamo first, because this is the place Carmelita has always wanted to see. Then they walk hand in hand across the street to an ice cream parlor. They take in the wonderful sights and rich history of this historical town.

They look at the bronze statues in parks throughout the town. The warm sun feels great on their backs, then the rain began. Then the sun peeks through the dark sky and the sun warms up to 90 degrees, then it rains again. They dash into the lobby with wet cloths and hair. The clerk behind the desk in the lobby gives them some advice, "If you don't like the weather, just wait five minutes." He laughs.

The Texas Ranger museum includes the Buckhorn Saloon, and a Bonnie and Clyde exhibition. They look at old photos, guns, badges, clothes, old newspaper clippings and wax figures. They eat a cowboy luncheon. Cody purchases three former Texas Ranger t-shirts for; his dad, Hansen, and Sam.

FATHERS UNITE

Tumbleweeds blow along the plains and thunder begins, the wind whips their hair and they take cover under an awning over a café. They sip sodas, and just as the man at the motel said, within minutes the sun comes out and the tumbleweeds cease to chase each other. Instantly the air is still and the sun is bright. You never know what you will get in San Antonio. They shake the water off their heads and continue to browse the city.

Before they left for San Antonio Cody's dad told his son, "Great place to visit. Enjoy your time away son, but prepare for all hell to break loose when you return. Prepare Carmelita too. Lea will not go softly into the night; you can bank on that." Ray slapped Cody on the back three times, pulled him in for a hug, then walked over and hugged his new daughter-in-law. Ray then stood back and gave her wink.

Sam is the chosen messenger. He seems the best choice—the deep voice of sanity. Sam agrees to tell Lea the news she has been asking for. Lea gulps and asks, "Who did Cody marry?"

Sam has to hold back the joy in his answer, he takes a second to clear his throat. Then prepares to state the fact. When Lea hears the name, "Carmelita," she goes berserk. Realizing that any reasonable conversation is over, Sam hangs up the phone.

Lea drives to the only place she thinks she can get answers; the ranch. She gets her sons out of the car, runs them into the bathroom, then tells them to play outside in the chicken coops. I brew calming tea and get some fresh baked bread then make sure Lea sits quietly and relaxes. She does sit, but you can see the steam coming off the top of

CHAPTER TWENTY-SIX

her head. Her chest heaves with every breath. She takes a few bites of zucchini bread, sips the tea, unaware it is a calming herb. She stands, and begins to ask questions and seems to be gaining momentum in her anger, much like a volcano. The cooks, Ramona, and younger sister Marie, listen from the kitchen. Hector and the other ranch hands also listen, as they pretend to weed next to the kitchen window. Lea's blood curdling boisterous yell comes from the main house, and scares the cattle. "Are you kidding me, he married Carmelita?" Lea takes a deep breath and screams, "He married the damn cook!"

I quietly take charge, "Yes, and she is a wonderful woman Lea, she has been here at the ranch for as long as I can remember actually long before I arrived."

Lea asks, "How long has this been going on?"

I reply, "How would anyone here possibly know the answer to that question?" I try and calm her down, "Lea Dear, you must get control of your emotions. Cody was a free man, yes he fathered your first child, but …"

Lea interrupts, "How the hell do you know about my personal life?"

I forge on giving it right back, "… that does not give you any rights in his relationships. Lea, he did not ask you to marry him, he asked a girl he's known most of his life. You need to show some class as you will be sharing custody with Cody and Josh."

Lea screams in a shrill voice, "What the hell are you rambling on about Nettie, this is crazy talk! Cody will never get my son."

FATHERS UNITE

I take a deep breath to prepare a comeback with both barrels and say my peace, when Sam quietly steps into the kitchen.

He stands taller than usual and walks right up to Lea, real close, past her comfort zone, "Lea, you need to stop, no one yells at my wife. You are in our home, you have caused enough trouble, you have hurt many people, now leave."

Lea busts into tears, "But Sam …"

Void of emotion he states, "After the boys have eaten you need to leave here, go someplace close by, those boys have been in the car far too long. Take them to a motel with a pool, they shouldn't be punished for this. Show some maturity girl."

Lea is not moving. Sam goes outside to retrieve the two young brothers, playing in the hen house—mostly chasing the chickens. He brings them inside and I bring them food and cold water.

Lea steps forward and says, "Come on boys, let's go."

Sam steps between her and the kitchen table and says in a firm voice no one has ever heard before. "They will be right along Lea, after they eat and tend to their business. Lea, if I ever hear, or suspect you are mistreating these young boys, I will come after you with everything I have, and then some." Sam steps real close to Lea, stands very still for a few tense seconds and says, "Now sit down and shut up."

Outside Hector looks at his men and gives thumbs up. In the kitchen the sisters want to hide inside a cabinet. But they quietly sit down at the end of a table and wait. They don't make a peep.

CHAPTER TWENTY-SIX

Lea backs away and sits at the end of the couch, smoldering.

The boys finish their grilled cheese sandwiches and bananas, drink some water then each runs into a bathroom, one upstairs, the other one next to the laundry room. They scurry back to the kitchen and I have cupcakes ready. Lea continues to sit and stare out the window. I step into the room and hand Lea a tall glass of water and some fruit and cheese. Lea accepts, but says nothing. She nibbles on the grapes and cheese and sips water. She never makes eye contact with Sam or me. Finally, the boys are ready to leave.

Cole and Zac are happy with full tummies. I hand each boy a book to look at on the long drive home. Lea is the last one out and leaves the screen door wide open, slamming against the side of the house as the wind catches it. She grabs her sons, puts them into their car seats and drives away.

We make sounds of relief. Sam acknowledges, "Cody and Josh got out of this one by the skin of their teeth. "Wine my dear?"

But unbeknownst to us, her anger is just the tip of the iceberg. Lea is not finished by a long shot.

Many months pass and Lea still tries to reconnect with Josh, but he is having no part of it. He admits he fell deeply in love with her, but because he was witness to her dark side, he keeps her at arm's length.

FATHERS UNITE

Jessica found out through an ultra sound she is having another girl. They are over the moon with joy and she and Archie agree on the name; *Robin Snow* after her mother and her mother's favorite singer Phoebe Snow.

Carmelita and Cody are living in DeSoto. Cody helps her with her English, but sometimes they speak in Spanish. Carmelita came home one day from an outing with her sister and the two happily prepared dinner. Later in the evening she arranges Cody's hands on her tummy and says, "Babe."

She tells him in English, but mixes it up with her Spanish, "Tres, and solo seis meses." He gets it. Cody gives her a joyful hug and understands it is not three babies in six months, and not six babies in three months. But one baby in six months. They are blissfully happy and as Carmelita grows in her pregnancy, so does Cody. Archie playfully suggests they hit the ranch and do some work outs. They love to meet up at the ranch; the brothers and all the kids play hard and get real dirty. This always results in an amazing time because Carmelita loves to cook, and the kitchen comes alive with her sisters when they arrive.

Sam and I take off once a year, to return to the scene of the crime—*the ocean*. We sit and watch the sunset and enjoy each other's company, and marvel how the two of us met under such odd circumstances. We don't run and fall into the ocean like we used to, well, we might fall in and roll around a bit, but no tossing.

Lea, has her hands full with raising her two rowdy sons. The noise and stress adds to her frustration from being divorced, feeling neglected and

CHAPTER TWENTY-SIX

dumped by Cody. Both boys are in school, and life becomes complicated, with custody and sharing schedules. Josh pays for both boys' child care, and he makes sure Cody gets his fair share with visitation. Cody sends Josh a check for Cole and Lea is none the wiser. Josh is open to Cody having custody of Cole, and sharing with Lea, as long as she keeps both boys when it's her turn, so they can grow up together. Cody and Carmelita have Cole once a month, and every third weekend they drive to the gulf to visit Josh, so the brothers can be together with two dads.

Lea tries to be agreeable because she wants Josh back. Lea has never forgiven Cody and he doesn't care. Lea toys with moving back to California but both Josh and Cody warn her that she will have the fight of a lifetime.

Jessica has found her balance in life. When she feels insecure, she'll lift the leather tabs and look into the trunk to reveal and remember the mother she never knew, who lost her life so young, and so avoidable. She thinks of her father with mixed emotions. She has tremendous appreciation for him giving her to me and great sadness for his incomplete life coupled with his disregard for life.

Archie is a rock, he and Jessica are a perfect match. With three children, they don't miss a step. Their home is comfortable, clean and many games are played outside and at the table, lots of art adorns their refrigerator.

Dana Bea and Coach, Charlie and Abby, Archie and Jessie all visit each other along with their kids frequently. They spend days at the lake, boating and cooling down.

Cody and Carmelita and their new baby girl Mona also join in, they all get along well, the guys toss the football, tackle each other while the women chase the kids. Coach has become the third brother. Many weekends are spent together. Sometimes this gang will make plans, call ahead and descend on the Ranch or meet at the lake.

Mona came into the world in a home delivery, with Carmelita's grandmother and her sister Ramona by her side. Their baby girl is beautiful with wide set blue eyes, very black hair and dark skin.

Sam and I playfully enjoy the simple things in life, like bird watching. We are always prepared for the next phone call or text about a new grandchild, or an emergency, or which family is on their way over. Whatever the news, we wait with open arms and always a warm meal. We like to hang out in our remodeled section of the original ranch house, with the new brightly painted tile with a Spanish style design. The furniture is overstuffed, and the sheer white curtains blow in the wind.

Many seasons are left to live in this home, with this family and the next generation to come. Dana Bea, Jessica, Carmelita and Lea have supplied many cousins to share stories as they grow up together.

The phone rings, there on the end of the line is Josh. He immediately dives in with a "Hi Dad, it's Josh. I need to talk to you about Lea." Sam sits down and tells Josh to tell him everything and asks what can he do.

"She is coming around and invites me to stay for dinner after I drop off the boys, I'm not sure what she is up to, I don't trust her."

Sam let's out a laugh and says, "Well son, welcome to the wonderful world of women. No one seems to understand their motives, except other women. I am sure of one thing, she has something on her mind, and let's just safely say, this girl has an agenda."

CHAPTER TWENTY-SIX

Sam gets serious and replies, "If I were in your shoes son, I'd ask her point blank, *What are you up to?* Tell her not to dance around in circles, ask her what's on her mind."

"She will get mad as women do when you question their good deeds, or she might act hurt because you don't trust her generous nature. Sam goes on. "I hate to toss you into a snake pit son, but you need to step up and realize; this is the woman who will raise your sons, the woman who will teach them about respect and honesty. You need to keep her on your good side, you get me? You make a good living son, but hold your cards real tight, and don't poke a stick at a snake."

Josh responds with a childlike question, "Dad is it possible for you to talk normal, without metaphors?"

Sam laughs and answers, "It's what I do. I'm a metaphor kind of guy Josh, what you need to do is pay attention, read between the lines, in other words, watch the road signs."

Josh is quiet, then laughs and says, "Okay, thanks, *I think,* and chuckles, thanks for making me think and observe. I get what you are saying about her, and so far she hasn't been the sweetest smelling rose in the garden."

"Right Josh, hell yeah, great metaphor," Sam joyfully tells his son.

We thought we had heard the last of it, but Lea does indeed have something up her sleeve. She has an attorney, and both Josh and Cody receive a certified letter on the same day.

Lea's plan is simple, for her anyway. She tells Josh he can have full custody of Zachery. She informs Cody, that with Josh's approval he can adopt Cole and have full custody. The foot note for her simple plan is this; she wants both boys; Cole and Zac for three weeks every summer and both boys every other Christmas. She informs them that she is moving to San Luis Obispo, California, and Josh and Cody must pay for the boys' flights there and back each year.

The fathers meet and hire their own attorney, all paperwork is clear and precise. All parties agreed. Cody and Carmelita adopt Cole and Josh not only gets custody of Zachery but finds a job in DeSoto, Texas. He and Cody have become great friends and they include Charlie and Sammy on many outings and sports events. Archie and Coach are included as well.

Lea never once spoke to Josh or Cody, all correspondence went through her attorney. When the paperwork was finalized she approved the travel schedules then she signed. She had Josh pick up their son Zac and all of his belongings. She had also packed up Cole's clothing and toys and gave Cole to Josh to deliver to Cody. When Cole arrives at Cody's home with his three boxes, Cody says one word under his breath, "Harsh."

Cole is too young to realize what is happening, but he is overjoyed to be with his other dad.

Josh and Cody phone Sam and me, Ray and Peg, Dana and Coach, Archie and Jessica for a sit down meeting about these turn of events. This *meeting* is a very animated discussion over great Mexican food with Margaritas and a few cold beers. Later in the day, Carmelita cooks with her sisters, and together they show Jessica and Dana Bea some of their kitchen secrets. Josh becomes the fourth brother.

CHAPTER TWENTY-SIX

Josh found a great house only a few blocks from Cody. His job is new and he is putting in long hours. He decides to make the boys his top priority and begins a new life. Carmelita helps Josh with childcare. Carmelita's sister Marie, lives with them and helps with baby Mona, the boys, and cooking. Everyone knows their place and job. No one mentions Lea or talks about the move. Deep down inside they all know Lea has just flown the coop, and left her sons behind so she can live the high life, and find another man.

Cody builds an addition onto their home. Lots of hammering and dust surrounds them. Carmelita and Marie pack up the baby, both boys and head to the ranch for a month.

Josh's business is expanding and he is making very good money. He asks Marie if she will help watch Zac in the evenings and prepare dinner for them. She happily obliges and walks Zachery to his dad's house in the late afternoon. All of this is a little complicated in the beginning months, but slowly everything begins to fall into place and feels natural.

Before you know it, spring, comes up on summer. The planned trip to California now seems like a bad idea. Sam and I step up and plan our annual trip to the coast at the same time the boys are scheduled to visit their mom. We decide to stay the full three weeks in California to make it easier on the families and the young brothers return home.

When Dana Bea stops by for a visit, Jessica comments, "She wasn't raised this way, I don't understand how she could let her sons go like that, she basically walked."

FATHERS UNITE

No one wants to slam Lea, what is the good in that, but Dana Bea can't help herself. She looks Jessica straight in the eyes and shares her observation. "Everyone knows Lea's parents cannot say no to her. Remember when we were getting ready to come to Texas the first time, for Mom and Sam's wedding? Lea had to come along too. Her parents said okay, with no questions about what we were planning to do or who would keep an eye on her. No one ever says no to Lea. But Cody did and Josh did, so she bolted back to her parents."

Jessie then realizes she is right, Lea always got her way, she always did whatever she wanted. "Thank you Aunt Dana Bea for opening my eyes."

A few weeks later a call came in to Jessica. It is her Aunt Rose who tells her, "Honey, your grandma Gladys passed away late last night. Jessica, she wrote you in her will. She left you her house, and everything inside. She also left you an undisclosed amount of money from her brother who left it to her in his will."

Jessica thanks her Aunt Rose and says, "I'll speak with Archie then decide what to do and when." Jessica cries for her sweet Granny and the lonely life she lived.

In late summer, before school begins, Archie, Cody and Coach fly to Medford Oregon, then drive to Yreka California. Jessie flies out with the men, but returns quickly to get back to her children. They are met by Rose who gives them a key and the name and phone number of the attorney. Sam and Ray fly out with Hector. Coach takes one day off to visit his family in Oregon.

CHAPTER TWENTY-SIX

The renovation begins as soon as Jessie shows them what goes to The Salvation Army and what is to be packed and sent to Texas. Everything is tagged.

The house is scraped and painted. Hector and Coach are all over the yard; repairing fences and replanting. The house is now the cutest one on the block and they find a realtor.

Rose stops by frequently with pizza and sodas and marvels at the speed at which these men work.

Rose is lost, sad and alone. She and Gladys had forged a deep friendship from a dysfunctional marriage of her brother Rich and Gladys' daughter Robin. Jessica toys with the notion of moving Rose to Weatherford.

Gladys stipulated in her will that after all of the attorney bills are paid, she wants Jessica to give Rose ten thousand dollars. The rest is for Jessie. Gladys' brother sold his orchards of walnuts and pears years ago, and Jessica acquired over four hundred thousand dollars.

The women in her life, her Aunt Dana Bea, Carmelita, and Nettie will each receive ten thousand dollars to do with as they please.

Gladys' house sells in five weeks. Jessica hires an accountant and gives all of the young children in the family a fund for college. Including Hector and Josh's children.

She also pays the guys who helped. Hector, Coach, Sam, Ray, Archie and Cody the sum of ten thousand dollars each for their work on Gladys' home. The remainder of her money she invests. Jessica also mails her dad a slush fund of five hundred dollars for cigarettes.

FATHERS UNITE

Jessica's life began with two wayward parents. Her life quickly escalated into a nightmare. Because of her father's admission to physical abuse coupled with an uncontrollable temper, he did the best he could do to save her. His life choices eventually drop into a downward spiral. He is resolved to pay a high price for the remainder of his life.

Jessica's addictive mother was doomed the day she met Rich. Jessica knew of no other life. She is lucky to have survived her first two years. She was marked the day she was born.

Yet, one day when the stars were all in alinement, everything fell into place; because of a conscientious neighbor with a nurturing spirit, and a will of steel.

Rose sells her home, has a yard sale, then packs up her belongings and moves to Weatherford, Texas. She finds a small bungalow in a senior complex, not far from Jessie and her family. There she has access to a warm pool, club house and many people her age.

Jessie's life takes a turn towards normalcy. She works hard, listens and learns. She grew to be a woman of warmth and courage. She will always and forever remember her sweet Granny Gladys.

Today, on her mantel sit two framed photos. One of her mother the other of her Uncle Joe.

CHAPTER TWENTY-SEVEN

A Breezy Day

I head upstairs, dirty from head to toe, wearing a pull over top, blue jeans and my well-worn red boots. Today Hector and I put the finishing touches on the vegetable gardens. We planted many varieties of peppers, summer squash, tomatoes, and beans. One section is for sunflowers. Hector surprised me by constructing a raised garden bed for the kids to tend. They plant watermelons and pumpkins.

The entire family is gathering this evening. I am excited to see Cody and Carmelita with young Cole, toddler Mona and baby Rex. Marie, her younger sister will be here with her husband Josh and son Zachery. Lupe looks forward to seeing her other daughter Ramona and proud papa Hector with their infant daughter Dominga, and older sister Caterina, whom they refer to as *Cat*.

I brush my long wavy hair; still thick and lush, although mostly white. I walk over to the balcony to watch the kids play in the side yard, in the shade of the large oak. Watching from my perch I pull my hair over my shoulder and begin to intertwine one thick braid.

CHAPTER TWENTY-SEVEN

Jessie lays on a quilt playing with her youngest daughter Robin, while her older daughter Jana is absorbed with her coloring book.

Jessie points up to the trees and says, "Girls, listen to the birds." Abby looks up, listens, and continues to brush her mom's hair.

"Shhhh, listen." Jessie whispers.

Jessica is a trusting woman and she never complains, and expects nothing. She is a strong girl with a sweet heart. Archie's compassion and strong will is instrumental in helping his wife's youthful scars heal, inside and out. Her life is complete and cherished.

Abby looks up into the shade of the tree and listens to the Meadowlark sing its special song. Jana Rose claps her hands and jumps up and down, but the bird doesn't fly away, it waits. The tree is silent, but not for long.

I am mesmerized by the amazing sunsets out here on the plains. I stand quietly and listen to the birds and gaze at the sun as it begins to set.

Sam saunters down the road after checking on some cattle. Behind him is his *gift*, who trails along. Last spring, Sam gifted himself a special day, *Sam's National Appreciation Day*. He named his gift, Louie. He requested no applause, but a big thank you was acceptable.

Here he comes, with his messy white hair that sparkles in the sunset. He looks hot and tired as he walks over to his old faithful bench and plunks himself down. Louie happily crawls under the bench and pops out between Sam's legs. Sam bends over and gives his new pal some nice long pats on the ribs and some pats on his head. He loves this

A BREEZY DAY

dog who checks the barn doors, corrals and chicken coops every night; to make sure everything is locked up tight. A silly dog for a silly man.

In no time Sam stands, stretches then takes a few steps across the path to be closer to the family. He sits back down on a well-worn huge stump, and wipes his head and chest with a bandana.

The kids play near their mothers. Dana Bea and Abby lay close and talk, enjoying the slight breeze that passes by. Charlie has some plastic army men, and Samuel has many sticks in a bag for the makings of a fort.

Sam senses my gaze and looks up. He grins with his crooked smile and nods yes. He pats his heart. I stroke my braid and smile back.

Sam smirks and says to himself, "I know what she is thinking—how much she loves me and she thinks I'm sexy no matter what I say."

"Incorrect Sam."

I look out across the plains and think; "I wish I could fly right off this balcony and soar across our ranch, over the horses, cattle, the gardens and the grandchildren at play. I would fly up into the oak and meet the other Meadowlarks and sing."

Sam tosses his head back and laughs. The girls look over towards Sam, then up to the balcony to witness me stretch my arms out with my head back, as if I might leap. The girls look to Sam; he opens up his arms as if to catch me. The girls watch him chuckle and continue to pet Louie.

A BREEZY DAY

Jessica and Dana Bea realize it's another one of our crazy flirtatious mind reading games. Jessie asks her aunt, "Do you ever wonder what they are really thinking?"

"Sometimes, but it's better to let things fly out into space and not clog our minds." Dana Bea answers with a laugh. Jessie giggles.

Jessica and Dana Bea lay together; taking in the warmth of the evening sun as it begins to turn gray with threatening clouds. They enjoy the songs from the Meadowlark while their minds go to a peaceful place.

Epilogue

IN NORTHERN CALIFORNIA the vibrant sun begins to set and change the majestic Mt. Shasta into an apricot glow. A new fresh face at the police station searches for things to do. His name is Brigg Kelly. He walks downstairs to the basement to take a look at stored cold case files. He thumbs through the files taking notice of dates and file names. One file with tattered edges stands out from the others: *1984, Holly Clute, Toddler.* He pulls this file out, and walks back upstairs. Slowly he flips through pages, reading details and the scribbled notes made by previous investigators.

Officer Kelly spends the remainder of his shift absorbing facts. His entire afternoon is spent in intense evaluation of the unsolved case. He draws charts using lines and arrows, from facts to possible leads. He scribbles his own notes, adds a question mark next to the names Richard and Robin. He attaches his notes with a paper clip.

This case needs someone to unravel it. Someone has missed a piece of the puzzle. Somewhere in the paperwork lies the key. Night closes in, officer Brigg Kelly places the Holly Clute file in the top left hand drawer of his desk. He'll resume tomorrow.

*The Meadowlark is known for its beautiful flutelike song.
You can listen to them sing out across a grassy meadow or a
field, and they can make anyone's day better.
These birds like to sit on fence posts, wires, along fences,
or hide in tall grass.
They are known to gather an audience
with their song, but are seldom seen.*

www.ingramcontent.com/pod-product-compliance
Lightning Source LLC
Chambersburg PA
CBHW071650090426
42738CB00009B/1482